RAINCOAST
CHRONICLES
18

STORIES AND HISTORY OF THE
BRITISH COLUMBIA
COAST

Edited by HOWARD WHITE
with PETER A. ROBSON

HARBOUR PUBLISHING

Harbour Publishing
P.O. Box 219
Madeira Park, BC V0N 2H0

Cover design, page design and composition by Martin Nichols, Lionheart Graphics.
Cover photograph of Pachena Point lighthouse by Chris Jaksa.

We acknowledge the financial support of the Government of Canada through the Book Publishing Industry Development Program and the Province of British Columbia through the British Columbia Arts Council for our publishing activities.

THE CANADA COUNCIL | LE CONSEIL DES ARTS
FOR THE ARTS | DU CANADA
SINCE 1957 | DEPUIS 1957

Printed and bound in Canada.

Canadian Cataloguing in Publication Data

Main entry under title:
    Raincoast chronicles 18

    ISBN 1-55017-171-2

    1. Pacific Coast (B.C.)—History. I. White, Howard, 1945- II.
    Title: Raincoast chronicles eighteen.

FC3803.R348 1998   971.1'1   C98-910224-6
F1087.5.R352 1998

Table of Contents

In the early 1960s, when Al Trice, Don Sorte and Mack Thomson went shopping for a submersible for their seat-of-the-pants diving and salvage business, they discovered that corporate giants like Grumman, Lockheed, Westinghouse Electric and General Dynamics were spending millions to develop commercial subs, but none was close to being on the market. With no capital and less experience, Trice, Sorte and Thomson's answer was to build their own.

In about 1919, when an official of the federal government arrives in Pender Harbour looking to collect taxes from an A-frame logger, he gets a lot more than he bargained for. More gumboot hijinks from master storyteller Dick Hammond, author of *Tales From Hidden Basin*.

There is no doubt that someone shelled BC's tallest lighthouse in 1942. Some say it was a Japanese submarine. Others suggest it was a covert operation undertaken by the federal government to unite Canada behind the war effort. Lasqueti Island writer Douglas Hamilton says they're all wet.

For sixteen-year-old Hal Dahlie, it was either stay in town and scrape barnacles or take a stint at the coast's most isolated light station with an old keeper who was more than a little strange. Dahlie chose the light and is still talking about it 50 years later.

Introduction

by Howard White

Apart from the odd rusting anchor on display in Vancouver and the lantern from the old Trial Island lighthouse in Victoria's Bastion Square, British Columbia is oddly devoid of maritime monuments for a province with one of the world's great coastlines. British Columbians can't be accused of wearing their marine heritage on their sleeves, but just the same, it's there interleaving the pages of our lives.

When Claus Botel brought his family from Germany to northern Vancouver Island in 1913, their homesteading tale turned into a story of sea adventure when their small boat shipwrecked them on Cape Cook. Botel's granddaughter Ruth Botel tells the whole story starting on page 46. Even a story of a determined tax collector pursuing an artless dodger turns into a boating story when it takes place on the coast and the scofflaw is a coastal gyppo. The taxman can only track him down by chartering Hal Hammond's gas boat out of Pender Harbour, as Hammond's son Dick recounts in "Svendson and the Taxman" (Page 19.)

With so much of our commerce dangling or floating over water, it should not perhaps be so surprising that BC would emerge as a leader in certain technologies like the self-dumping log barge, whose origins David Conn traces in "Booting the Big Ones Home." Nor, given the typical west coast disregard for authority, should it be surprising that in 1963, when three hungry Vancouver scuba divers were told their idea of building the first commercial salvage sub was beyond the capability of all but the world's largest hi-tech manufacturing corporations, they went ahead and tried to do it on a shoestring. What is a little surprising, as Tom Henry describes in "*Pisces* Ascending" (page 7) is that Al Trice, Don Sorte and Mack Thomson should succeed so brilliantly, establishing BC as a world leader in submersible technology.

One way to get the saltwater boiling in west coasters' blood is to threaten the coast's much beloved lighthouses, as several automation-minded politicians have found to their sorrow. So it shouldn't be surprising that the one event of World War Two still being hotly debated on the west coast is the alleged Japanese shelling of Estevan Point lighthouse. In his book *Keepers of the Light* (Harbour Publishing 1985), lighthouse historian Don Graham contended that the shelling was a hoax perpetrated by the Canadian government to rally support for conscription. In this issue, Lasqueti Island writer Douglas Hamilton returns fire.

Few people carry around with them a stronger sense of the role the sea plays in our lives than commercial fishermen. Hank McBride went to work in the fishing fleet in 1937 when he was fourteen and still does relief duty as skipper on some of the coast's larger draggers and packers. He loves to tell stories, and the stories he tells bear witness to a free and unfettered sea-going lifestyle that has now all but vanished from the coast, as Michael Skog recounts on page 68.

Here on the BC coast, nobody thinks to make a big noise about the sea and its influence on our lives. But when we stop to think, it's all around us.

Pisces Ascending
The Little Sub That Could

by Tom Henry and Ken Dinsley, photos and illustrations courtesy Al Trice

Under the scudding grey clouds of a December morning in 1966, a small workboat towing a wooden scow laboured out of Burrard Inlet, under the great span of Lions Gate Bridge, and set an unsure northwest course into the Strait of Georgia. The little procession was unremarkable in the context of Vancouver's busy port, with its swarming harbour tugs and hulking freighters, though a few experienced seamen did pause to note the incongruity of the obviously underpowered boat struggling with its cumbersome tow. Probably a gyppo logger on a rubber-cheque budget. They blew into Vancouver and scoured the harbour of its marine dreck—the paid-off barges, the fire-sale boats—then bulled them up coast. These seat-of-the-pants mariners, it was said, were either ballsy or brainless. Many thought they were both.

A more colossal incongruity was apparent to the crew of the little workboat. As the *Hudson Explorer* ground past Point Atkinson and leaned into the long, slow pull to Jervis Inlet, they had time to reflect on the magnitude of what they were about to attempt: the first manned deep-water test of their made-in-Vancouver submersible, named *Pisces I*. If successful, they would hurtle past corporate giants like Grumman, Lockheed and Westinghouse, which were all pitching millions of dollars into the race to build the world's first commercially viable non-military submarine.

For twenty-six months, three Vancouver divers, Al Trice, Don Sorte and Mack Thomson, working under the name of International Hydrodynamics Ltd. (HYCo), had struggled to complete *Pisces I*, a teardrop-shaped submarine perched on the lumbering scow. They needed to prove the sub could descend to 600 metres, with a pilot. It was this depth that the US Navy had decreed the vessel must be able to achieve if HYCo wanted in on lucrative work recovering sunken torpedoes from the Maritime Experimental Test Range at Nanoose Bay on the east coast of Vancouver Island. With the *Pisces* project hopelessly over budget, the torpedo recovery contract was a Holy Grail to HYCo. Complete the test and they could pay down their crippling debt, land other Navy contracts, and sell their vessel's technology as the most versatile, affordable salvage sub design in the world. Fail to reach 600 metres and not only would they fulfill the predictions of all the experts who said the sub would never work, but a) one of them would very likely be steak tartare at the bottom of the sea and b) the other two would be commercial diving for the next twenty years to pay off their debts.

In spite of the impressive ring of the name, International Hydrodynamics was anything but a large corporation. It consisted of the three partners: the president, who could not read or write; the designer, whose idea of research consisted of thumbing through back issues of *Popular Mechanics*; and the general manager, who seriously listed as credentials for building a submarine an incomplete apprenticeship building wooden hulls at one of the oldest boatyards on the coast. Filling out the staff of HYCo were a deckhand (who doubled as a bouncer when paycheques were scarce), a secretary and three poodles.

The three poodles belonged to Don Sorte. Sorte (pronounced Sor-tee, or Sor-gee to some) was sometime president of HYCo (in its early days the company did not get tangled in corporate order) and chief spokesperson. For this latter task he was admirably gifted. He was 6'2", exotically handsome, and fond of attention-getting stunts such as hurling off his toupee while dancing at Vancouver's fabled Cave night club. (He kept a table at the Cave, though he did not drink or smoke.) Sorte also loved to flash wads of hundred-dollar bills, which may or may not have had something to do with the non-stop company of impossibly buxom women at his side.

If money and spectacle didn't get attention, then his poodles did. Sorte often dyed the dogs different colours (rose, blue and yellow being favourites) and took them out on business, including visits to the service counters of banks. All three dogs answered to the name Tiger.

"That way," Sorte once explained in his confident, booming way, "I had to yell once and all three came."

For all the bravado, however, Sorte was remarkably secretive. His life was sandwiched between an uncertain birthday in an uncertain part of the USA, and a mysterious death (or at least disappearance) in 1977, while sailing across the Indian Ocean. In dozens of interviews he never gave the same information twice about his age. (If you take the average of the many birthdates he gave to the Vancouver press during construction of *Pisces*, Sorte was probably thirty-eight in 1966.)

Sorte had a lifelong love of money which ultimately, and ironically, led him into the money-gobbling *Pisces* project. This passion may have been the product of a destitute youth. Sorte had a near-phobic dislike of poverty: faced with taking a one-light-bulb room in a cheap hotel or sleeping in his car, he'd choose the car. He was raised in the American Northwest and got a start in business in 1953 by placing what became a controversial ad in a Seattle newspaper—"We will do anything day or night, Don or Mc," followed by a phone number. He was twenty-five, married with two children, and continually short of money.

Sorte was a fan of scuba diving, which in the 1950s was still in its infancy. He was attracted to the frontier aspect of diving: very likely, in the early days, he was looking at a scene no human being had looked at before. Soon, Sorte realized diving was a potential moneymaker. He took a miscellany of underwater jobs, including a regular gig recovering accident victims from submerged automobiles. The police, all too aware of Sorte's immoral imperatives, advised him to stay out of victims' pockets: they needed the wallets for identification.

With no training or experience, Sorte and his partner Mc took on contracts to salvage sunken logs from freshwater booming grounds. Their approach made up in simplicity what it lacked in sophistication. With a heavy set of tongs attached to a crane, they rowed or waded into the water and slammed the tongs into a log. The crane then pulled the log onto land. The water, of course, quickly filled with sludge and goop dragged from the bottom, so they worked by feel, slithering through piles of slime-covered logs on the lake bottom.

If the pile shifted, the men could be trapped or crushed. It was a lucrative business, though, and lasted until Sorte broke up with his wife and moved to Vancouver with a new girlfriend.

Sorte's chance to break into the closed shop of the BC commercial diving scene came in June 1958, when a span of the Second Narrows Bridge collapsed, killing eighteen workers. During attempts to recover bodies trapped in the wreckage, a commercial diver was lost as well when he was carried off by the tidal rip. Whether or not because of the accident—Sorte felt it was—the divers' union opened its doors a crack and Sorte was inducted into the Brotherhood of Local 2404 of the Pile Drivers, Bridge, Dock and Wharf Builders of Vancouver, as a commercial diver.

Sorte became an excellent diver and was paid well. The money was good because the odds of even a small accident turning serious were bad. But diving was dangerous, too. During one job Sorte worked on, a supposedly routine hard-hat chore cleaning up under a Vancouver pier, his air supply was accidentally cut off. The intake hose from the compressor, always placed upwind and well away from the exhaust fumes of the motor, had been left hanging near the surface of the water. Spray was sucked into the hose, shunted down to Sorte by the compressor and detected by the sensor in his helmet. The sensor, designed to cope with a completely severed air hose, immediately clamped shut the air valve in Sorte's helmet. No water was going to get in, but neither was any air. Sorte heard the clunk of the air valve shutting and knew instantly what it was.

"They tell you there is a five-minute air supply inside your helmet but I find you tend to black out after three minutes," Sorte recalled. "I began gathering up all my hoses and such to move out where I would be clear to be drawn up by my tender. I kept calling out to him on my voice line, 'George, are you up there? George! Where are you, George?'"

George was away momentarily, getting coffee.

Sorte regained consciousness flat on his back on the wharf with George slapping his face and crying at him to wake up.

With his diving earnings Sorte bought a home, complete with pool, in the toney British Properties in West Vancouver. He cruised town in flashy cars. He even had an oil painting commissioned: it portrayed a man kneeling in adoration before a huge dollar bill. "One thing about Sorgee," a friend explained, "you didn't take him seriously, you just experienced him."

Sorte met Al Trice through his diving work. Trice, a soft-spoken, pipe-smoking Steve McQueen look-alike, was an early member of the divers' union—and a longstanding regular in Vancouver's waterfront community. After a brief attempt, in his teens, to manufacture wooden sailboats, he drifted through a variety of maritime jobs: fish boat deckhand, towboat skipper and finally, a job as apprentice shipwright at the venerable Mercers Star Shipyard in Queensborough. "Everything

Two of the originators of the *Pisces* submersibles, Don Sorte and Al Trice, in their hard-hat diving gear.

was big—the hammers, the chisels the planes—everything," Trice recalls. "They used to say, 'If it isn't hard work, it isn't Mercers.'"

The yard was not graced by anything that might be called technology. There were no cranes. It took three weeks to put a 2,000-kilo engine in a boat. As Trice explains, "Together with your helper—just one, you always had just one helper—you wedged it up, built a bridge across the deck of the boat, levered it over, then eased it down into the engine room. Scared to death the whole time the thing would get away on you. It was like building the pyramids."

All this was conducted under the eye of Mercers' temperamental foreman. "If you're going to smoke," he once declared to Trice "you're going to smoke tailor-made. You're not rolling on my time."

In May 1953, Trice met Keith Carter, an ex-British Navy frogman. Within a week Carter took Trice diving and Trice was hooked. This, he knew, was his calling. Trice especially enjoyed the three-dimensional freedom of diving—where "up" and "down" lost meaning. He and Carter formed a business, hoping to promote scuba as an alternative to the more prevalent hard-hat diving. But hard-hat divers were intractable. They referred to the aqualung as "mouse gear" and the divers who used it as "frogs." Trice's attempts to sell Vancouver on the merits of the new diving technology failed, and the business folded. But his diving career flourished. By 1964 Trice was one of the most respected commercial divers in the Lower Mainland. That year he was called on to make some of the riskiest dives of his life.

In early spring, *Barge 10*, loaded with heavy bunker "C" oil, turned turtle in heavy seas and sank near Pasley Island in Howe Sound. Trice was asked to do the salvage survey. Compounding the usual dangers of salvage work was the fact that Trice would be diving alone to depths of at least 80 metres. Jacques Cousteau, the French underwater pioneer who essentially made scubas accessible, stated in a book published in 1963 that 61 metres was the maximum depth for, as he called them, "aqualungers." Divers were still using ordinary air, which is 79 percent nitrogen. (Nitrogen gas enters the bloodstream under pressure and is responsible for the crippling, sometimes fatal, bends divers can get when they surface too quickly.) Trice says, "You did lots of dives to 80 metres alone. They wouldn't pay for two divers. That's all there was to it. Some dives you just have to back out of. You just can't do that dive. You'd get too narc'd."

"Narc'd" refers to the other problem dissolved nitrogen causes: nitrogen narcosis, whose effects are often quoted in martini equivalents. For each 20 metres a diver descends, the amount of nitrogen forced into the bloodstream by the increasing atmospheric pressure has an impact roughly equivalent to drinking one martini. At 100 metres, or after pounding five quick martinis, a diver's thought processes become confused. He does foolish things, like offering his aqualung to passing fish or remaining on bottom long after his dwindling air supply should have sent him back to the surface.

Working alone, Trice completed his survey of the wreck. He discovered *Barge 10* was leaking. In his report he noted the barge lay on a slope with its shallow end at a depth of 80 metres and the deep end at 100 metres. Even at 80 metres, each minute a diver spends on bottom requires corresponding minutes of decompression time at various stops while returning to the surface. The difference in depth between the two ends of the barge was only 20 metres, but each of those metres added dramatically to the decompression time. The problem was going to be air supply: a diver needed enough to descend, work, then make the long, slow ascent.

Trice, Sorte and another diver were contracted to do the underwater work. It was to be the deepest diver salvage operation ever undertaken, hard-hat or scuba—anywhere on the west coast. Trice and Sorte had been to such depths only a few times prior to the work on the *Barge 10*. These were sporting test dives off Vancouver's North Shore. The men had done a so-called "bounce" dive, going down to 100 metres and straight back. (Years later a good friend of Trice's drifted to the surface dead after a much shallower bounce dive.)

The underwater work on *Barge 10* proved more difficult than Trice or Sorte had anticipated. After several twenty-five-minute dives at the work site, they had to reduce bottom time to fourteen minutes per dive.

Fourteen minutes was just enough time to secure a shackle or work a pin into place. Then it was time to make for the surface, following a carefully planned schedule. On the support ship they scrambled out of oil-coated suits and into a decompression chamber, where they often slept for hours. They shortened their work schedule to four days on and three off and still they were exhausted.

The *Barge 10* job was successful, but it convinced Sorte and Trice that they needed a submarine. Just as the aqualung freed the hard-hat diver from his awkward gear, so a submarine would free the diver from all the hazards associated with working at extreme depths. A sub would double or even triple the diver's range of operations. The men's ideas were fueled by the fact that Cousteau's submarine *Denise*—or *Diving Saucer*, as she was also known—and her surface support ship *Calypso* were in operation off the coast of California in early 1964, receiving a lot of media and trade journal coverage.

One morning shortly after the salvage of *Barge 10*, Trice appeared in front of Sorte's posh West Vancouver home and announced he was heading south to look at submarines. Sorte didn't even pause. He shot inside, crammed a toothbrush in one pocket and a bulging wallet in another, and the two headed off on an unusual shopping trip.

Now, at lunchtime on that December day in 1966, the *Hudson Explorer* and the scow entered the deep waters near Captain Island, in Jervis Inlet. As Sorte and Trice brought the *Explorer* alongside the barge, HYCo's third partner, Mack Thomson, got ready to go down in the submersible. Unlike hard-hat or scuba diving, work in a submersible requires no special gear. For the occasion, Thomson, 5'8", 135 pounds, had troubled to don his favourite 007 James Bond sweatshirt. Nor did *Pisces* require a lot of preparation: its batteries were charged, its oxygen tanks filled. The only thing that distinguished this dive from many others—besides the extraordinary depth—were the web of stress wires stretching across the submersible's crew chamber. These wires measured microscopic changes in the sphere's dimensions via change in the wires' electrical

resistance. For Thomson, this was an unusual concession to technology. Ever the make-doer, he had tested the hull of the *Pisces* in its first unmanned submersions by lashing pieces of wooden lath together. If the sphere contracted while submerged, the laths slid past one another and Thomson was able to measure the difference when the craft returned to the surface. To date, *Pisces* had exceeded everyone's expectations.

Moving with practised ease, Thomson clambered into the *Pisces* crew chamber and secured the hatch. Outside, the cable from the scow's on-deck crane was hooked to the submersible and it was hoisted over the side. The descent to 600 metres was scheduled to take several hours. Without complicated decompression stages to go through, the craft simply drifted down to the designated depth; then, after blowing water ballast with compressed air, it returned to the surface.

Prior to building *Pisces*, Mack Thomson's closest formal contact with submarines was the Wednesday evening meetings of the Seattle contingent of the US Submarine Naval Reserves. He had joined the reserves not because he was interested in submarines—he was more interested in boats—but because it was an alternative to being drafted into two years of military service. In his four years with the reserves, he never once went down in a submarine. Sea duty consisted of a few cruises in small navy ships on Seattle's Lake Union, during which Thomson was occasionally allowed a turn at the helm. He was told to "steady up on Grandma's Cookies"—a large billboard at the head of the bay. The assignment that carried the greatest burden of responsibility was to teach knot-tying to a more junior class. As soon as his obligatory time was up, he resigned.

Thomson was a nudist and a spiritual brother to Zen mechanic Robert Pirsig, in the sense that he had a near-spiritual affinity for matters technical. "Mack sometimes thinks something, and then, to him, it *is*," said Trice. "He doesn't differentiate."

Like Sorte and Trice, Thomson first got into scuba diving as a sport. Too broke to buy a dry suit, he made his own rudimentary outfit by gluing and stitching together yards of the material used to protect baby mattresses. By wearing a full set of woollen long johns under this plastic suit, he was able to tolerate the frigid waters of Puget Sound. He acquired a secondhand regulator, then made his own K-valve to fit the breathing apparatus to his air tank.

Thomson's inventiveness blossomed in the frontier world of scuba diving. Using salvaged parts, he manufactured an underwater lighting system that, for the first time, enabled photographs to be taken at depths of greater than 10 metres (approximately the limits of full-spectrum light). He showed some of his photos to Don McKuen of KOMO TV, who hosted a popular program called "Exploration Northwest." McKuen was so taken by the photos, and by Thomson's contagious enthusiasm, that they teamed up to produce several programs, one of which garnered the station a prestigious Sylvania Award.

Occasionally inventive beyond recklessness, Thomson once thought he had found a nifty way to ascend from the depths by blowing up his suit like a balloon and rocketing to the surface. A horrendous case of the bends arrested further development of that idea.

Thomson was one of those guys who read technical and trade magazines. In one of these journals he came across an account of how Washington's Grand Coulee Dam was regularly inspected by hard-hat divers. It was risky work. The dam is one of the largest in the world—the waterfall over its spillway is 107 metres wide and falls more than 50 metres—and the terrific currents in and around the areas to be inspected were extremely hard on divers in their cumbersome gear.

Thomson concocted the idea of doing the inspections in modified scuba gear, and immediately focussed all his exuberance in a drive to convince some fellow divers it could be done. Instead of the bulky hard-hat suits, they would use seamless wet suits made—in typical Thomson style—by pouring rubber over manikins. Each diver would wear a small tank of air for emergencies. Connecting them to the surface would be air, hose, telephone and safety lines. With the increased mobility, Thomson reasoned, they could do the inspections much more quickly and much more cheaply than hard-hat divers.

Thomson's bid on the job was successful. The inspection was done in September, when the water level in the dam was as low as possible. The giant turbines were slowed to a minimum and the divers went to work. The water was absolutely clear, so much so that Thomson, working from a platform halfway down the inside of the dam, had an attack of vertigo. He felt he would tumble through the water to the bottom of the dam.

Thomson met Sorte and Trice in Seattle in 1965, at the home of a mutual friend. Trice and Sorte were on the way home from their shopping trip, unimpressed by what they had seen. American Submarine Company of Ohio and Perry Submarine Builders of Florida had both built subs that could dive to 30 metres, but neither was designed for salvage work. In California, Trice and Sorte had visited corporate giants Westinghouse Electric, General Dynamics and General Mills—all working on submersibles—and in every case were welcomed more as colleagues than potential competitors. Executives began calling the Canadians "the T-shirt boys," because of their casual attire. Despite or perhaps because of their unprofessional appearance, Trice and Sorte were ushered into the deepest recesses of the security-conscious research laboratories. (At Lockheed's aerospace research centre they were allowed to watch a prototype moon buggy being put to the test.) Although boggled by the technological excesses of the American submersible programs, Trice and Sorte did note many practical features which they would like to see in a submersible. These ideas would prove invaluable in the future.

Even when they looked beyond North America, the only other sub remotely close to their needs was Cousteau's *Denise*, completed in 1959. A prototype, it was described as "a scrutinizer, a loiterer, a deliberator, a taster of little scenes as well as big," but it was not on the market.

The remaining option was to build a sub, but that too sounded unfeasible. Before leaving Vancouver, Trice had run the idea of building a sub by an engineer at Patterson Boiler Works. "The man was very nice. He sat down with us and carefully explained why building a submersible was impossible." Despondent, Sorte and

Trice asked Thomson if he could build them a sub. Thomson said yes.

Thomson's first step in the design of the sub was to inhale as much of the literature as possible. Among the many texts he consumed was the account of a Swiss man named Jacques Piccard, one of the foremost authorities on submersible design at that time. In 1960, four years before Thomson started on his sub, Piccard, backed by the French Navy, reached a depth of 11 kilometres in a submersible named *Trieste*. The dive, which set a depth record that still stands, was made in the south Pacific Ocean, in a trench named the Challenger Deep. The overall design of *Trieste*, which employed an enormous bag of gasoline to lift the sub to the surface, was totally impractical for a salvage sub, but Piccard's account was invaluable. In particular, Thomson noted Piccard's advice that "the cabin is the vital part of any deep ship; around it all other components must be fashioned."

A submersible's cabin must be capable of withstanding tremendous pressures while keeping its crew not only dry, but at the same atmospheric pressure they left at the surface. The pressure on every square centimetre of the cabin's outside surface increases at a rate of approximately one-tenth of a kilogram per metre of depth. At a depth of 1,000 metres, the pressure is over 100 kilograms per square centimetre. (In Imperial measures: over 1,459 psi.)

The hull design with the smallest surface area—at least the shape which mathematically optimizes the weight-displacement ratio and distributes the pressure most evenly over the surface—is a sphere. Ottis Barton's bathysphere, in which he and William Beebe were lowered on a tether to an ocean depth of 930 metres in 1934, was a metre and a half in diameter, which gave them space enough to see if they could do it, but not enough to provide a working environment for a salvage job. Thomson knew his sub would need room for two crew, plus masses of equipment.

When asked where he had got his information about hull design and materials, Thomson explained: "We just ask our friends. We've got lots of friends who give us information." One of those friends was Warren Joslyn, one of Boeing Aircraft's top stress engineers. Josyln's original contribution to the project was the terse delivery of the comment that the project was impossible. Then, snared by Thomson's limitless enthusiasm (as many, many others would be), he began designing. The engineering specs he prepared for Thomson called for the submersible to be built around two spheres, a larger one for the crew and a smaller one containing various tanks. It would be capable of submersion to 500 metres. Vancouver Iron and Engineering contracted to build the sphere. Thomson took office space in their shop, and the long job of bending metal began in the summer of 1965.

After six months of relentless work, the frame and two spheres were completed. The bill was almost $50,000, thus cleaning out HYCo's entire budget. (The US Navy had paid $50,000 for a submersible named *Intelligent Whale*—in 1872!) HYCo moved *Pisces* from the fabricators to an unused space in the back of a mushroom cannery in east Vancouver. They secured the space in return for helping load crates of tinned mushrooms onto trucks.

Power, steering and breathing systems were completed, but slowly, as Thomson often worked without benefit of engineering drawings. (Incredibly, *Pisces I* was built from a total of forty-four drawings, about the same number, an engineer claimed, needed to build a coat hanger.) Thomson built many parts himself, often at home in the evening. The next day he would show his handiwork to Trice, who would find a way to drop it on the warehouse floor. If the part broke it wasn't any good; if it didn't break, it had passed the *Pisces* quality test.

Originally, HYCo's partners had hoped for the sub to be ready in three months (and $20,000). After fifteen months, Trice and Sorte, in the depths of debt, insisted on seeing the sub tested in the water. Thomson, who had an inventor's disregard for time and budget, said he wasn't quite ready. They would have to wait. By this time *Pisces* had been moved into a little shack at the end of Vancouver Pile Driving's pier in North Vancouver. Desperate to see how their investment was going to perform, Trice and Sorte waited until Thomson was away, ran *Pisces* out on the I-beam and lowered her into the ocean. The submersible did not float straight at all; the

The twin spheres of *Pisces I* were fabricated for HYCo by Vancouver Iron and Engineering.
L to r, Al Trice, Mack Thomson and Don Sorte.

tail end sank. Sorte, who was never big on reining in his emotions, developed a case of the financial bends, declaring the whole venture had been an enormous waste. When Thomson returned, they confronted him with the sub's problem. Thomson was typically philosophical. "Oh well," he said. "We learned a lot." This sent Sorte into even greater paroxysms of anger and frustration. He had been taking every diving job that came along in order to finance the sub, and it wouldn't even float straight. It fell to Trice to defuse the situation. "What are we going to do?" he deadpanned. "I don't know; give up." Disgusted, Sorte and Thomson agreed to carry on.

"There's no magic," says Trice, who has an engineer's patience for mechanical problems. "You can only use what's there. We're always asking for magic. There is no magic."

The problem of *Pisces'* heavy tail proved easy to solve. Thomson bought two hundred Grimsby troll floats at a nearby commercial fishing store and crammed them into every accessible tail section of *Pisces'* fairing. Each float had 3 kilograms' lift and was good to a depth of no less than 525 metres.

Among other problems plaguing the emerging submersible was arc and fire—or, in HYCo lingo, "A & F"—in the electrical system. Electrical problems became so common they were spoken of lightheartedly, but shadowing the jokes was the memory of a fire of catastrophic consequences on board one of Jacques Cousteau's test subs, caused by a short. The sub was quickly lifted onto the deck of the *Calypso*, but when the fire couldn't be put out with carbon dioxide foam it was dropped back into the sea. If there was a serious fire in *Pisces* while Thomson was aboard, even alongside the docks, there was no one to yard the sub out of the water quickly. Testing was a serious business, or at least it was supposed to be.

Thomson often worked on *Pisces'* interior while it was submerged off VPD's dock. With a radio blasting, he painted the hull aquamarine and white, then set to installing an infinity of controls. The chronic shortage of money led to continual compromises. For example, the scrubbers that controlled the critical level of carbon dioxide in the air were driven by a sewing machine motor. Thomson had lifted it from his wife's Singer during a conjugal visit to Seattle. He did splurge on a telephone, which he hooked up inside *Pisces* to save himself the bother of having to clamber in and out whenever he needed to call for parts or advice. People on the other end of the line, listening to Thomson's voice echoing and re-echoing, jokingly asked if he was inside a well. He replied that he was sitting at the bottom of Burrard Inlet.

The final stages of work on *Pisces I* took place in this shed at the end of Vancouver Pile Driving's pier in North Vancouver.

In the mountainous confines of Jervis Inlet, the crew would need more than a phone line to stay in touch with Thomson, particularly at the depths he intended to reach during the dive. Underwater communication equipment was only marginally effective in those days. Radio waves could not be used, as they spread out rapidly in water and soon became unintelligible. *Pisces'* communication was based on sound. Sound can travel for hundreds of kilometres in water if the conditions are right, but refraction can be a problem; sometimes the sound bends as it travels. As the effect of refraction is minimized on the vertical plane, it was imperative the *Explorer* sit directly above *Pisces*.

Complicating the problems of communication was the proximity of a US Navy vessel also in Jervis Inlet.

After contacting the ship—an innocuous-looking buoy tender—the crew of the *Hudson Explorer* was alarmed to discover it was testing a new generation of anti-submarine torpedo. These torpedoes were being fired out a tube on the stern of the ship, then whizzing away in search of underwater targets.

Thomson irreverently radioed the US ship, explained what HYCo was about to do and asked them to postpone torpedo tests. The Americans, working to schedule, were reluctant to cancel their tests, but stopped just short of refusing. They may have recalled an incident that had occurred before the testing of the American submersible *Deepstar 4000*. Her support boat was mistaken for a target by a Navy ship and had three 5-inch projectiles dropped 200 metres astern of her before she was able to advise the Navy of their error.

The HYCo team and the US Navy ship established what they considered to be a reasonably safe distance between them. It was also agreed the Navy would advise HYCo when they were about to fire a torpedo by raising a

On a cloudy day in December of 1966, Mack Thomson prepared for *Pisces I*'s first test dive to 600 metres in the waters of Jervis Inlet.

red flag. This signal was a near-useless concession as the torpedoes were fired from the deck of the ship: the HYCo crew could watch the launches through binoculars.

During what was supposed to be a long break in the torpedo tests, *Pisces* began its descent. Crouched below the stress wires, Thomson guided the vessel under the surface as easily as he would back his car out of the garage. By this time the fantastic and foreign treats of underwater travel were familiar to Thomson. To the few guests who had been down in *Pisces*, even to relatively shallow depths, it was like a trip to a new world. One American fisheries expert, a guest on a dive in Puget Sound, had taken along a tape recorder and a camera. So dazzled was he by the first-time sight of the rich waters that, as Thomson gleefully noted, he spent much of his time talking into his camera's light meter and pointing his microphone out the view port.

Thomson's first checkpoint was at 170 metres. He reported all was well, although the response from the *Hudson Explorer* was garbled. On the surface, the crew of the *Explorer* were having equal difficulty understanding Thomson's scratchy reports. To Trice, the communication problem hinted at a more serious situation. He realized they were no longer directly above the sub; *Pisces* had drifted out from under them—and toward the torpedo target.

As Thomson continued with his descent someone on board the *Explorer* noticed a red flag raised on the Navy boat. There was no time to call off the dive. Warren Joslyn, along for the ride, tried frantically to advise the Navy to hold the fire, but they suddenly seemed to develop communication problems of their own. Trice advised Thomson to shut everything off aboard *Pisces*. Then, with gut-wrenching horror, the crew of the *Hudson Explorer* watched a torpedo shoot from the deck of the Navy ship, splash into the water and hurtle away.

Far below, Thomson had been recording his thoughts and observations on a tape recorder. He had heard enough of the squawking message from the *Hudson Explorer* to realize his predicament. He shut down all unessential electrical gear. *Pisces* was now still and silent. Thomson even clapped his hand over his wristwatch to muffle its ticking. He left the tape recorder running and on the tape one can distinctly hear the whine of the torpedo's screws as it cuts through the water seeking a target—exactly as Thomson heard it, crouched in the sub, alone, 200 metres underwater, waiting for any change in tone to indicate the torpedo had homed in on *Pisces*. Even though the torpedo was unarmed, he knew it was a toss-up whether it would impale *Pisces* or pass right through.

After an unbearably long time, the sound of the torpedo trailed off and Thomson continued the dive. When he paused at 330 metres to take stress readings there seemed no particular problem other than the discovery that he had lost all communication with the surface. Normally, this would have been cause to call off the dive, but after the business with the torpedo the loss of communication didn't seem that serious to Thomson. Besides, HYCo didn't do things normally.

Shortly after *Pisces* passed the 400-metre mark, an explosion jarred Thomson from the controls and the sub plunged downwards. Thomson's first reaction was to leap up, thus becoming snarled in the strain wires. Fighting to free himself, he struggled with controls to blow the ballast tanks and arrest the descent. There was the familiar hiss of compressed air and gurgle of bubbles as the tanks were cleared, but *Pisces* did not respond. She continued to sink. Thomson could see particles like dust motes, illuminated by the 1,000-watt headlights, snowing upward outside the viewing ports.

Down *Pisces* went, level but uncontrolled, like a feather wafting from a nest. While the depth gauge recorded his plunge toward the bottom, Thomson considered his options. There remained only one possible way *Pisces* was going to return to the surface: releasing an untested 185-kilogram drop weight would have to compensate for whatever buoyancy was lost in the explosion. Had the drop weight mechanism been damaged in the blast?

An emergency drop weight is exactly what it sounds like; a weight that can be dropped from the sub if a large and sudden increase in buoyancy is needed. On *Pisces*, the drop weight was held to the frame by a long, finely threaded crank. Thomson's struggle to release the weight was recorded on tape.

"Fourteen hundred feet and still descending. (Creak, creak, pant, puff, puff.)

"Fifteen hundred feet and still descending. (Puff, puff, puff.)

"Sixteen hundred feet and still descending."

Finally, the weight fell away.

"Thank Christ," said Thomson, to no one. "It's gone."

At this point *Pisces* should have shot up like a bubble. It did not. It merely slowed in its descent. What Thomson had failed to take into account was Archimedes' principle; an engineer had suggested a drop weight of 185 kilos in water. He had made the weight 185 kilos on land.

Still *Pisces* continued to sink, though Thomson, with desperate optimism, thought it might be descending more slowly. Down, down it drifted for another 30

metres, where it came to a standstill, suspended in the black waters. Thomson studied the depth gauge. Six hundred metres. *Pisces* had reached the test depth. But would it rise? *Pisces*' searchlight sent a core into the dark water, but there was nothing to indicate whether the craft was going to hold steady or ascend. Thomson shivered in the chill cabin. The hull ticked under the tremendous pressure.

Again Thomson peered at the depth gauge and considered his immediate future. *Pisces*, designed to take two and even three passengers on day-long expeditions, had enough oxygen to last for forty-eight hours. If Thomson shut down all systems and tried to conserve air, he might last for sixty hours. After that, he knew, would come shortness of breath and blackout. While considering his fate, he kept his eyes on the depth gauge. Slowly, like a minute hand on a watch, the gauge indicated the sub was rising. Thomson could only keep his eye on the controls, and hope there would be no more catastrophes.

Far above on the surface, daylight was dwindling. The US Navy vessel had discreetly concluded its tests and steamed away, leaving the *Hudson Explorer* alone in the inlet. It had been hours since last contact with *Pisces*. With night falling, the crew realized soon there wouldn't be enough light to take bearings. They would be unable to hold *Explorer* over the spot where *Pisces* had descended. Trice ran the boat to the nearby shore, where the scow was secured, and started the power plant to provide light for a reference point. Then all they could do was return to the approximate place where *Pisces* had gone down and wait helplessly for the sub to reappear. Other than to refill a cup of coffee, or search for yet another pack of cigarettes, no one could move. The group huddled on deck, scanning the waters for any sign of *Pisces*. If it did surface, it was important they spot it quickly. *Pisces* rode so low in the water that, between evening winds and tidal currents, it could easily drift away, unnoticed, for miles. The American submersible *Ben Franklin* had drifted six hours on the surface before her support ship located her. Another, named *Alvin*, had been lost for ten hours off Bermuda.

They need not have worried. From the black waters came a light some of the crew later described as an atomic bomb going off, and which others felt was a near religious experience. It was dim for a moment only, then burst into brightness in the black stillness of the waters. It was *Pisces* ascending, led by its powerful headlights. The submersible bobbed to the surface. It was midnight. Thomson had been down for eight hours.

What had caused *Pisces* to sink was an explosion—actually an implosion—of such force it had torn a portion of the fibreglass from the fairing and sucked it into the hole of one of the four smaller 40-centimetre spheres used for ballast and trim control. Thomson had been lucky. If even one more of the spheres had gone, releasing the drop weight might well have been futile. But Thomson was jubilant. The ballast sphere was a simple thing to replace, and *Pisces*, as far as he and the military needed to know, were good to 600 metres.

Although they had no way of knowing it at the time, *Pisces'* inventors had launched a technological renaissance in BC. Success of the little submersible on the torpedo range, and in subsequent salvage operations, led to the building of more *Pisces* crafts—ten in all. International corporations—including some who had entertained the "T-shirt boys," yet failed to complete their own subs—noted the upstarts, and within a few years *Pisces* versions were working on cable-laying projects in the Atlantic and capping oil wells in the North Sea. Experts from all over the world came to visit, including scientists from the USSR, one of whom went on to lead an underwater exploration of the *Titanic*. As HYCo grew, so did the support industries around it—a plethora of Lower Mainland firms specializing in underwater communication, propulsion, navigation and remote control vehicles.

Mack Thomson emerges from *Pisces I* after the near-disastrous test dive.

Unfortunately the profit side of HYCo never proved as buoyant as their submersibles. Some of this was the fault of the owners, who insisted on redesigning the sub every time they received an order. Some was the fault of the Trudeau government, which, when HYCo signed a crucial multi-million-dollar deal to sell subs to the USSR, gave in to American pressure and revoked the company's export permit. After fifteen years—from 1964 to 1979—HYCo folded as a business, although its subs, in the hands of other firms, continue to work to this day. So do its former employees, many of whom own and manage firms in Vancouver's elite underwater research firms. Among this crowd, HYCo is referred to as the "kindergarten"—the place where it all began.

But back on the wooden scow that December night in 1966, all that mattered to Trice, Sorte and Thomson was that their idea had worked. As they toasted *Pisces* and each other with glasses of champagne, they swapped jokes about how those aboard the *Hudson Explorer* had debated pouring that same bubbly into the water as a memorial to Thomson. They secured *Pisces* and made ready for the long, slow haul back to Vancouver. For their success they had only themselves to thank. And, perhaps, an American torpedo with lousy ears. ◆

Tom Henry is the author of The Good Company, *a history of the Union Steamship Co. (Harbour Publishing, 1994).* Pisces Ascending *is from* Westcoasters: the Boats That Built BC, *coming soon from Harbour Publishing.*

Svendson and the Tax Man

by Dick Hammond

Father was working on his boat at the dock in Pender Harbour. This wasn't at all unusual. The owner of an old wooden boat can, if he wishes, spend most of his spare time at this, and Father was fussy about maintenance. The year, probably 1919. Perhaps 1920.

The *Cassiar* had docked and was loading freight and passengers. Immersed in his repair job, Father paid little attention, until there came the hard sound of leather soles on wood. He looked around to see a stranger approach and stop. A cadaverous man, middle-aged, neatly dressed in dark suit and darker tie, a raincoat folded over his left arm. He wore severe-looking rimless glasses and peered through them at the young man rather as if he were examining a bug that was new to him.

"Are you Mr. Hal Hammond?" he asked, in a soft smooth voice.

Father said thoughtfully, "It could be two men you're looking for. One of them's known as Hal; then there's a Mr. Hammond..."

The man regarded him with an icy stare.

"You were pointed out to me as being Mr. Hal Hammond. Now, what kind of foolishness are you up to? Are you, or are you not, he?"

"You look like a government official to me," said Father coolly. "A lawyer friend of mine told me never to admit anything to government officials. But just supposing I was this Hal Hammond, what would you be wanting him for?"

"Lawyers!" sniffed the other contemptuously. "A useful tool but they need watching. As to why I am here, I need transportation and I was told that you could supply it."

"I think," said Father cautiously, "that could be arranged. Just where do you want to go?"

"There is a man called Svendson, who operates, I believe, a logging camp somewhere in the vicinity. I wish to see him on government business. Do you know his whereabouts?"

Illustration by Alistair Anderson

"I know Svendson. He has a camp up in the inlet. I can take you … Take about two hours to get there, though."

Time seemed no worry to the stranger. He agreed readily to the fee, and before long, they were heading up the channel toward Jervis Inlet.

When some time had passed in silence, Father tried a few conversational gambits. They generated only the minimum response. But then the other produced one of his own.

"This Svendson, does he have a profitable business?"

Father considered this, and answered that he really couldn't say.

After a few more tries, the man tried another tack. "A nice boat you have here. Does it bring you much income?"

Some instinct of self-defence stirred in Father's mind, as he hedged, "Oh, I make just enough to pay for fuel and repairs."

The stranger looked dubious. "Then it would not appear to be worthwhile to do it, if that's the case?"

"No," agreed Father blandly, "probably not worthwhile. But it's a living."

There was a long silence as the man turned this over in his mind a few times. His long face assumed the expression of one who has found something in his soup, but hasn't quite decided to call the waiter. He sat there silently, and Father made no more attempts to communicate, so the rest of the trip was made in silence.

At last, Svendson's A-frame came into view, and Father steered in toward it. An A-frame consists of a couple of long trees, usually on a float. They are tied together at the top, but spread wide at the bottom to give stability. Cross braces make it look more or less like an A, and support wires—guy lines—hold it upright. A heavy wire goes from a machine on the float, through a pulley on the peak of the A, and up the sidehill into the woods. Many of the steeper parts of the coast were logged in this way. A-frames can be quite efficient. Svendson's was not one of these.

There was no sign of activity as they eased into the float alongside Svendson's old boat, but as he was tying up, Father saw the man they were looking for appear

out of the shed that held the machine. He came across the logs to greet them, wiping his hands on his clothes as he came. Of average build, he was balding, but made up for that with an unusually thick moustache. He wore the usual caulk boots and heavy pants with wide braces, but no shirt, only the grey Stanfield underwear worn by most loggers. This was almost as much hole as cloth, and out of the holes on his chest stuck tufts of hair of the same light brown as that on his lip and scalp. There was black grease smeared on his head and face, and two broad strips of it on his chest where he wiped his hands.

"Hello, Hal." He put out blackened hands. "Guess what I've been doing. Machine's down again." Looking at the man in the expensive suit, he said, "Who's your friend? I'm afraid I'm not hiring at the moment." His eyes twinkled as he almost grinned.

Father, out of his passenger's line of sight, rolled his eyes and shrugged his shoulders eloquently, as the man made his way carefully across the deck of Svendson's boat and onto the big logs of the A-frame float.

Safely there, he said with some dignity, "I assume you are Mr. Svendson? I am not applying for employment, sir. My name is Turner." He held out his hand, but on seeing the state of Svendson's, withdrew it protectively to his pocket. "I represent the government of Canada. To be more specific, the income tax department."

(Income tax had been imposed in 1917 as a wartime measure, with the assurance that it was only temporary. It is said that people actually believed this!)

Svendson withdrew the proffered hand.

"Income tax? What do you mean, income tax?"

"You should know, Mr. Svendson, as a businessman, that you, and all people earning over a certain amount of income, are required to pay a tax on it, as of 1917."

"Ay be not busynessman, ay be logger. Ay make no money, ay pay no tax." Svendson had suddenly acquired an accent. As Father well knew, this was a device that allowed Svendson to misunderstand whenever he chose, and thus give him time to think. He had honed it to a fine point on persistent creditors.

The tax man said patiently, "That may be so, Mr. Svendson, but you must file the papers to prove it. There are no papers filed by you since the tax was imposed. None at all."

Svendson shook his head. "Ay file saws. Ay not file paper. Vat do you mean, file paper?" He squinted his eyes and pursed his lips, which made him look like a caricature Swede.

"Mr. Svendson, I must remind you that this is a serious matter. I am here to audit your books, and to determine how much money you owe the government. Now, show me your office, and we can begin."

"Office?" countered the Swede. "Vot do you tink I am, a doctor? Dere is no office, no books—unless you vant my girlie magazine—and I owe the government notting! Vat has de government done for me, that I should give dem money? Vill you tell me dat, Mr. government man?"

"Why, there is the army to maintain, for one thing. A war is very expensive you know."

"De var is over. For vy do ve need an army? Und dey said de tax vas only till de var vas over."

"Well," said the other firmly, "I'm afraid it's going to last a bit longer. The government needs money to help the country become prosperous. And there's the police, the mail service, the roads..."

"I saw a policeman vunce," mused Svendson, "at a dance. He was drunk. I haf no car, and for de mail, I buy stamps. Und, if de government takes people's money, how can dey be prosperous?"

"But you may want to buy a car, and then there will be roads to drive on."

"Den I vill pay de gas tax, vot is for to build de roads."

By this time, the accountant, having forgotten his original purpose, was now determined to justify his employers. He said earnestly, "Mr. Svendson, you must realize that running a country costs a great deal of money. There are construction works; the parliament buildings, for example. There are a great many government employees who must be paid. People must pay taxes, Mr. Svendson."

But Svendson was having none of it. "By Yeesus, you are right about costing money! Vat do dey need big rock houses for to sit in anyhow. And dere's a lot too many

people vorking for de government should have an honest job, instead of going around bothering oder people vot are trying to earn a living."

This rather low blow had its effect. His opponent flushed, and went on the attack.

"People must pay taxes," he insisted hotly. "You can't just take from the country, Mr. Svendson, you must also give something to it." But Svendson was more than ready for this one.

"I pay stumpage tax on every tree, Mr. Turner, and yust about everyting I buy, the government's got a finger in it somehow. And as for de country, vy vere vould it be witout people like me? De towing boats get vork, de carpenters vot use de vood get vork. Und nailmakers, und hardvare, und everybody. Und vot do I get?" He put a finger in one of the holes in his Stanfields, and out another. "Dese here are my best pair. De other is a bit vorn. And now, ven I make a bit of money to keep, you say dey are going to take some of it away!"

The tax man, taken aback perhaps as much by the decrepit state of Svendson's underwear as by its owner's rebuttal, actually appeared to be sympathetic. "But you should realize, Mr. Svendson, that you are not very likely to have to pay a large amount of tax. In fact, I would estimate that it is not at all likely to exceed ten percent of your net income. You surely must admit that one dollar out of ten is not very much to give for the running of your country."

"It was the wrong thing to say," laughed Father. "Up until now, the talk had been sort of theoretical. Not real, but now it was down to earth; it was real dollars that were coming out of Svendson's pocket. Out of every ten dollars, he was going to lose one, if the tax man was right!"

Svendson blinked with shock. He lost every trace of accent as he said in disbelief, "Ten percent! Ten dollars out of every hundred! Do you mean to stand there and tell me that out of every thousand dollars that I make, they are going to take away one hundred?" As the sums mentioned grew larger, Svendson's voice grew louder, more incredulous.

"Well, not exactly," said the gaunt man in his precise way. "The rate rises with the amount earned—" Then, seeing Svendson's face, he added hastily, "but there is a tax-free minimum, you know."

But Svendson was considering something, and didn't appear to have heard the last bit. "Do you mean to say that some big shot banker that makes a million dollars will have to pay more than a hundred thousand dollars of it to the government?"

The accountant actually smiled at such naiveté, an expression that ill suited his long cadaverous face. "Oh, well, Mr. Svendson. We must be realistic about these things. The wealthy have resources that are not available to people like us."

Svendson nodded thoughtfully. "Yes," he murmured. "I thought so. And what will happen, Mr. tax man, if I don't pay these taxes?"

The other man looked shocked at such a heretical notion. "Why, they will seize your goods, all you own. They will take your machine there, and your logs. You could even go to jail!"

Svendson nodded again, and appeared to come to some decision. "Wait there," he said, with the air of one who has been relieved of a burden. "I'll be right with you. I just have to call my two men."

He turned and went over to the shed, from which a piercing whistle sounded. A shout from up on the hill replied. There was a slight delay, then he reappeared, carrying a battered suitcase. He was now wearing a shirt. "I'll just be a minute. I have to tell the men what's going on, then I'll be ready to go."

"Go, Mr. Svendson? Where are you going?"

"Why, to jail, of course." He waved his hand comprehensively. "She's all yours. Tell the government they can have it, every bit of it. It's not worth a thing. The engine won't run, the lines are shot and the timber's rotten; I've got no money, so I guess it's jail." He seemed quite cheerful about the prospect, rather like someone heading out on a picnic.

"Now, wait a moment, Mr. Svendson. I'm sure you are being too hasty. This isn't at all necessary, you know."

But Svendson had made his mind up.

"I want to go to jail," he insisted. "I need a rest." He held out his hands. "I work my fingers till my hair falls out, and what for? So's someone can take the little bit of money I put by."

"But, ten percent, maybe less, it's not so much to get all excited about."

"Only ten percent, you say. But just look here, Mr. tax man. After a working man has paid for all he needs, about all he has left over is ten percent of what he makes, so what you are asking for is really one hundred percent, and I am not going to pay it!" Svendson's mood had changed. He was now waving his arms and shouting, causing the other to look nervously behind him, making sure of the path back to the boat.

"Take me to jail!" shouted Svendson, red-faced. "I insist you take me to jail. Three meals a day and no worries. A roof that don't leak and no damn engines to break down. I want to go to jail!"

By this time the accountant had made his way across the cluttered deck of Svendson's boat to the comparative safety of Father's. He said, low-voiced but urgently, "Hurry, let's get out of here, the man's gone crazy. You don't know what he might do. Hurry up, he may come after us!"

Svendson was now on the deck of his boat, still shouting that he wanted to go to jail, that the government could have everything.

"Wait for me," he pleaded, as Father shoved off. But he seemed oddly slow in covering the short distance to Father's boat. Then Father shoved the clutch in, and they glided swiftly away as the boat gathered speed. The tax man's back was turned, and he stared resolutely down the inlet to where lay civilization. Father looked back. Svendson was standing on the deck of his boat, waving happily. There was a big grin under the bushy moustache. ◆

Dick Hammond is the author of Tales From Hidden Basin *(Harbour Publishing, 1996). Svendson and the Tax Man was excerpted from Dick Hammond's second collection of tales, coming soon from Harbour Publishing.*

Who Shot Estevan Light?
A Traditionalist Returns Fire

by Douglas Hamilton

As summer's dusk settled slowly over the lighthouse at Estevan Point on that memorable night of June 20, 1942, keeper Robert Lally happened to stare out to sea. In the distance, off to the southwest, he made out a "warship zigzagging under heavy smokescreen." The sight was not uncommon during the early days of the war as Canadian naval crews based at Esquimalt frequently trained in these waters. But when the shells began to fly at the big light, Lally realized that this was no training mission. Within minutes of the attack, the keeper had rushed up the 45-metre lighthouse tower and extinguished the powerful beacon. He then stepped out on to the cupola and, from this ringside seat, observed the attack in detail. The shells arrived, at first 500 metres out, then 350, closer and closer. At least six shells landed in front of the light, while others roared over the tower like "freight trains passing over a bridge" and exploded near the Native village of Hesquiat. In all, about seventeen large shells were fired, although some

Looking inland at the Estevan Point light tower. Buildings are painted wartime grey. The fog alarm building is next to the tower and the Lally residence is to the left. *(photo by Robert Lally, circa 1942)*

The evidence suggests that the Japanese submarine *I-26* shelled Estevan Point lighthouse in 1942. The vessel was destroyed near Leyte Gulf in November of 1944 by American Navy planes.

observers later reported as many as twenty-five. Witnesses were unclear as to how many vessels took part in the shelling; many identified the attacker as a large submarine, probably Japanese; some thought they saw other ships as well. There were no injuries and damage was surprisingly slight: only a few windows in the tower were broken by flying debris. The terrified Natives at Hesquiat fled by boat into the protection of Hesquiat harbour. Civilians at the lighthouse were evacuated into the darkening bush in case of a land invasion, while the rest of the staff stolidly remained at their posts.

Fears of a landing party or demolition squad proved groundless: the intruder vanished as silently as he had arrived. Over the next few weeks, authorities examined the evidence, including craters, metal fragments and a dud shell. It was quickly concluded that the fire had come from the 14-cm gun of a Japanese submarine— the first enemy attack on Canadian soil since the War of 1812. Defences at the isolated lighthouse were beefed up and life soon returned to normal there. The matter rested for more than forty years.

Then, in 1985, lightkeeper Donald Graham published *Keepers of the Light*, a book about British Columbia's lighthouses that soon became a classic. In his chapter on the Estevan Point lighthouse, he argued convincingly that the attack had had nothing to do with a Japanese submarine. Some eyewitnesses had claimed that at least two large vessels were conducting the shelling, but Graham ridiculed the notion that the Estevan light was a credible military target for anyone. In fact, he argued that it would actually be an aid to enemy navigators. And how could the "gunners get twenty-five straight misses around that huge 150-foot tower, sticking out like a clay pipe in a shooting gallery?"

Japanese B-1 submarines had a hangar and catapult forward of the conning tower for launching seaplanes. During its 1942 voyage to Vancouver Island, the *I-26* used the hangar to carry supplies instead of a float plane. (*illustration courtesy* Retaliation)

No, it was not the Japanese. Rather, Graham suggested, it was a covert operation undertaken by the federal government (perhaps in collusion with the United States) to unite Canada firmly behind the war effort. Canadian or American warships fired those shells harmlessly to scare the bejesus out of Canadians, and in particular, to wake up those reluctant Québecois and other "lukewarm patriots" to the very real dangers of the deepening war. Shadowy RCMP officers reportedly threatened dismissal or prison terms to any witnesses at Estevan who disputed the official version of the incident. The dud shell bore Japanese ideographs in yellow paint, but according to Graham, the lightkeeper also claimed that English "markings, numerals and whatever" were stamped on the base of the shell. And the entry for June 20, 1942 in Lally's official lightkeeper's logbook has mysteriously disappeared. Even the American intelligence personnel who compiled the official record after the war, using confiscated Japanese documents, felt the sting of Graham's contempt. Commander Yokoda's description of submarine *I-26*'s attack on Estevan was summarily dismissed as a sore loser's evil nonsense: "Yokoda was a questionable confessor at best. There's no more despicable trade in warfare than commanding a submarine. It takes a man with a shrivelled soul to peer through a periscope, put the profile of an unarmed merchant ship on the open sea behind the cross hairs, and order torpedoes away. He can be sure there won't be many survivors."

To cap this argument, Graham pointed out that on June 19, the day before the attack, Parliament was debating a contentious amendment to the 1940 National Mobilization Act which would have permitted conscription. The shelling of Estevan was, he claims, used with great effect by proponents of the amendment, and was instrumental in allowing the bill to pass final reading in July.

This "Great Canadian Conspiracy Theory" soon took on a life of its own. In 1994, CBC-TV aired a segment on "Fifth Estate" that featured Donald Graham. Linden MacIntyre, host of the show, also interviewed two witnesses to the shelling: Myna Peet, then eight years old, and Robert Lally, Jr., about the same age. Then

MacIntyre observed: "The Americans even trotted out a submarine commander, Minoru Yokoda, who boasted that he directed the shelling of Estevan Point…For Donald Graham it boils down to a test of credibility. The war stories of a defeated Japanese submarine commander, against the eyewitness account of a lightkeeper with nothing to gain from embellishing what he saw."

It is not surprising that many Canadians believe the attack on Estevan was a grand manipulation, an event staged by agents provocateurs—courtesy of the Canadian government.

Does this hypothesis hold up under careful scrutiny? There is a considerable body of evidence, ignored by both Donald Graham and "Fifth Estate," that a Japanese submarine did attack Estevan lighthouse that night.

A number of daring raids on the west coast of North America were carried out by Japanese submarines in 1942. The effects were minimal, but the attacks represented a serious effort by the Imperial Japanese Navy to cause disruption along the west coast and to sow fear and confusion. Within weeks after the bombing of Pearl Harbor, according to Bert Webber's book *Retaliation: Japanese Attacks and Allied Countermeasures on the Pacific Coast in World War II*, no fewer than nine Japanese submarines had arrived off the west coast to attack shipping vessels moving between the Juan de Fuca Strait and San Diego. Only a handful of cargo ships were sunk before the Allies greatly increased their antisubmarine vigilance. Intense air and ship patrols made life so difficult for the Japanese raiders that military officials in Tokyo decided to take a more drastic step: direct attacks on the coast. On the evening of February 23, 1942, the Imperial Navy submarine *I-17* surfaced off of Santa Barbara, California. Commander Kozo Nishino took the vessel past the resort town and up the Santa Barbara Channel for about 30 kilometres to Ellwood, coming abreast of the Barnsdale Oil Company oil fields at about 7:00 p.m. The sub was only 1.5 km from shore when it lobbed twenty-five 14-cm shells at the oil installations in the space of twenty minutes.

On board *I-17*, the nine-man gun crew under gunnery officer Lieutenant Shimada worked methodically

Built in 1909, the 150-foot Estevan Point lighthouse was not only one of the tallest free-standing concrete structures in the West at the time, but as historian Donald Graham wrote, "the boldest, most beautiful lighthouse in all British Columbia." *(photo by Robert Lally)*

This unexploded 14-cm shell from *I-26* was found in a pile of driftwood after the attack. *(photo courtesy Robert Lally)*

loading, aiming and firing their heavy weapon, while anti-aircraft crews, expecting an air attack at any moment, hovered nervously over two 25-mm machine guns. When the shelling ended, the big sub headed west and slipped silently out to sea. According to Webber's *Retaliation*, US Navy radio operators intercepted a coded report sent to Emperor Hirohito later that night which claimed that Santa Barbara was "a seething mass of flame, with wild panic visible onshore."

Miraculously, damage to the refinery was estimated at only $500. Two dozen oil workers escaped unhurt and no fires were started. A pier, oil derrick and local land values were the only casualties. But fear is quickly contagious, and panic erupted across Los Angeles the next evening as jittery anti-aircraft crews cruised the skies searching for Japanese bombers. On the way home, *I-17* sank two cargo ships within a week. The Allies had their revenge: eighteen months later, on August 19, 1943, *I-17*

met her end off New Caledonia during a running surface battle with a New Zealand minesweeper and two US Navy planes. Out of a crew of ninety-four, six were rescued.

Four months later, according to the *New York Times*, the Imperial Navy shrewdly planned a double hit to achieve maximum psychological effect: Estevan was to be shelled on June 20 by Captain Minoru Yokoda and the crew of *I-26*, and on the next night, Fort Stevens, a US Army fort at the mouth of the Columbia River near Astoria, Oregon, was to be shelled by Meiji Tagami and the crew of *I-25*.

The attack on Estevan was carried out on June 20 as scheduled. The following evening at 11:30 p.m., shells pasted the beach between Fort Stevens and the small vacation community of Seaside, Oregon, leaving seventeen 1.5-m craters. Captain Tagami of *I-25* began firing from an extreme range of 13,000 metres, with a water depth of only 30 m. Because he was using a very old American chart, he mistakenly thought that the fort housed a submarine base. Tagami was also unaware that Battery Russell had the only operational 10-inch (25-cm) guns at Fort Stevens. Fortunately for him they were not pressed into service that night: little damage was done to the base. Nearby residents of Astoria were shaken from their beds by the loud explosions, and hundreds of people watched a spectacular light show far out at sea each time the gun fired. But instead of panicking, most witnesses seemed to revel in the excitement. "The Japs picked a swell place for harmless target practice," one resident commented cheerfully to a reporter. Colonel Doney, spokesman for the US Army, unequivocally blamed a submarine for the attack. He noted that the shell fragments found in the craters had come from high-velocity, low-trajectory shells which appeared to have been fired from several kilometres offshore. The sub drifted or sailed about 5 km during the bombardment. Doney added that an air search for the invader was under way. That search was unsuccessful.

Just hours after the incident in Oregon and barely a day after the shelling at Estevan, Radio Tokyo trumpeted a great naval victory over Canada and America. According to Domei, the official radio news agency of wartime Japan, important military installations in both countries had been destroyed by submarine bombardment, causing dismay and confusion along the entire defence perimeter of the west coast. Citizens from Alaska to Mexico were "panic stricken" by the attacks on Seaside and Estevan, and Canada in particular had been taught a painful lesson. Shelling the lighthouse was but "the first blow at the Canadian mainland…Thus Canada has been shown she is attacked by the Axis navies from the East as well as the West." The story pointed out that Estevan lay very close to Puget Sound and numerous important military bases; more raids should be expected. The attacks were so devastating, said the report, that the Allies would no longer be able to send supplies to Australia, and further air raids on the Japanese mainland were now completely out of the question. Japanese submarines in combination with the

Edward T. Redford found and photographed this unexploded 14-cm shell two weeks after the attack.
(*photo courtesy* Retaliation)

German U-boats in the Atlantic would also cut off supplies to the Russians, thereby preventing the opening of a second front in Europe. These claims were of course inflated into the hyperbole of wartime. But if the attack on Estevan came from Canada's own navy (with the possible help of the Americans), how would the propaganda spin masters at Domei, thousands of miles away, have found out the details so quickly, and used the information with such excellent timing?

The most audacious wartime attacks on North American soil were launched in September 1942. Japanese naval designers had long been fascinated by the idea of a submarine capable of carrying and launching an airplane. The I series, B class submarines used in all of the west coast attacks were very large cruising boats, each with a watertight airplane hangar fore of the conning tower. They were over 105 metres in length, they displaced 3,300 tonnes, and with a range of 25,000 km they could remain at sea for ninety days without servicing. As well, a small float plane provided eyes for the sub (there was no radar on Japan's submarines until much later).

Code-named GLEN by the Allies, the little float plane was a marvel of compactness and ingenuity. The fuselage, wings, floats and fins were detachable and divided into twelve connecting pieces. Flaps and tail folded neatly to fit into the cramped cylindrical hangar fore of the conning tower. Powered by a small 340-hp radial engine, the stubby plane had a top speed of 150 knots and an endurance of about five hours. Its battle load consisted of a small machine gun and two 76-kg bombs—if intercepted, GLEN would have been no match for Allied fighters. Preparation for launching via the compressed air catapult took a tedious hour, as did recovery which was carried out with a special crane located on the foredeck.

Following the attacks on Estevan and Seaside, the two submarines returned to Yokosuka submarine base in Japan for supplies. Then, according to Flight Warrant Officer Nobuo Fujita, *I-25* sailed back to the west coast in early September for what Japan hoped would be the most provocative attacks of all. At dawn on September 9, Fujita loaded two incendiary bombs onto his float plane and catapulted off the deck of *I-25*. Accompanied by petty officer Shoji Okuda, he flew his GLEN low over the well-lighted Oregon coast, dropping his bombs in the large forests 80 km inland near Brookings, Oregon. An alert forest ranger noticed the mysterious dawn raider, with an engine that sounded like a "Model A Ford hitting on three cylinders." He quickly located and doused the flames. When the float plane returned to the waiting sub, it was taken aboard just in time. An American A-29 Hudson bomber with British markings had sighted *I-25*; it dove and straddled the vessel with 135-kg bombs. *I-25* was severely shaken, but only lightly damaged.

Three weeks later Fujita repeated his air attack 18 km east of Port Orford, Oregon at around midnight. There is no confirmation that the bombs even exploded, and no fires spread into the damp underbrush. Fujita, who had experienced the Doolittle bombing raid firsthand in April 1942, later recalled: "That pilot had bombed my homeland for its first time. Now I was bombing his. It gave me great satisfaction." On their return flight, the aviators were led astray by a malfunctioning compass.

> Suddenly I remembered our compass trouble after the Sidney [Australia] reconnaissance. I pulled the Zero [not to be confused with the famous Zero fighter] into a quick turn, and headed directly for the Cape Blanco lighthouse. It could mean interception, but I didn't care. At least I could then die gloriously, crashing into an enemy plane. I might even dive into the lighthouse. Anything, to do the enemy damage through my death, and make it mean something, rather than just waiting for death to find me.

Instead, at the last minute, the two crew members decided to try once more to rendezvous 40 km offshore. Fortunately *I-25* was leaking a streak of oil, which led them to the sub and thus saved their lives.

For some months after the Port Orford incident, the Americans remained puzzled about the little float plane. Almost all civilians of Japanese descent had been interned in resettlement camps in the distant interior;

there was concern that some had been missed. Could the GLEN have been launched from one of the countless lakes in the Pacific Northwest—final proof of a fifth column of Japanese traitors loose on the mainland? Weeks of hard slogging through the bush produced no results. A searcher reported: "We found beautiful mountains, beautiful lakes, good fishing, tall wonderful trees, and mosquitoes and sore, wet feet. We didn't find any Japs." On July 11, 1943, *I-25* was sunk in the Solomon Islands by the American destroyer USS *Taylor*.

Since the first wave of doubt immediately after the Santa Barbara/Fort Stevens shellings and Fujita's bombings, no one has suggested that they were anything other than the work of Japanese submarines. The evidence on both sides of the Pacific is irrefutable. It should not be so

Minoru Yokoda, commander of *I-26*, remembers the night of the attack: "Because of the dark, our gun crew had difficulty in making the shots effective. At first the shells were way too short—not reaching the shore. I remember vividly my yelling at them, 'Raise the gun! Raise the gun!'"
(photo courtesy Retaliation*)*

difficult to believe that the very similar attack on Estevan was also made by the Imperial Navy—especially when veteran Japanese submariners themselves confirm it. In researching *Retaliation,* author Bert Webber made every effort to contact surviving Japanese submariners in the early 1970s and to get them to talk about the war. Most of them had been killed in battle, and some of those who survived were reluctant to talk about their experiences because western writers had misquoted them and treated them with contempt. But Webber did interview several retired Japanese submariners, including Commander Minoru Yokoda of *I-26,* who remained silent until 1973. But his memory of the Estevan shelling was still clear.

> It was evening when I shelled the area with about 17 shots. Because of the dark, our gun crew had difficulty in making the shots effective. At first the shells were way too short—not reaching shore. I remember vividly my yelling at them, Raise the gun! Raise the gun! to shoot at a higher angle. Then the shells went too far over the little community toward the hilly area. Even out at sea we could hear the pigs squealing as shells exploded. [Yokoda may have heard harbour seals, which bark, bray, hoot and bellow when disturbed.] As I watched from the *I-26,* the people were very quick to put out the lights in the buildings but the lighthouse was slow to respond—the last light to turn off.

There is no "boasting" in this fascinating account, as Donald Graham suggests. On the contrary, the mission was a great disappointment to the Japanese commander, as he freely admitted. "There was not a single effective hit that night," he said. Similar stories were told by Nubuo Fujita and Commander Meiji Tagami of *I-25,* among others, and details of their stories have been corroborated by surviving crew members.

The Great Canadian Conspiracy theorists have glossed over or ignored other inconsistencies. First, the Estevan lighthouse was no small mom-and-pop operation in 1942. On the night of the shelling, there were twenty-two people at the isolated outpost—seventeen of them staff. The *New York Times* described Estevan as "one of the largest radio centers on the coast." It housed a telegraph, weather centre, lighthouse and powerful radio station to co-ordinate shipping throughout the north Pacific. The *Victoria Daily Times* observed: "The irony of the shelling of Estevan lies in the fact that for the past 30 peacetime years the Estevan radio station has been giving complete radio services broadcasting weather conditions and handling air traffic generally for Japanese steamships which before the war were regularly operating in the trans-Pacific route."

In fact, Estevan was an excellent military target, and the real question is why Canadian authorities had failed to realize this earlier and provide it with more protection.

Second, if the shelling of Estevan had been an elaborate setup designed to garner support for the war, local governments would have been informed of the ploy and would have made a big fuss over it. But just the opposite was true. After two days of headlines, the matter almost disappeared from view in both Canada and the USA. The mayor of Victoria remarked a day after the attack, "I haven't noticed any change in the people's demeanor…no one is jittery. Why should they be over a nuisance raid such as Estevan or Seaside?" When BC Premier John Hart was asked by reporters if he would issue a message calling for calm, he tartly responded, "No one has the jitters and it would be ridiculous to suggest they needed such a message." Even the *Toronto Globe and Mail* played it down. "This first attack on Canadian soil failed to cause any great excitement on the West Coast made war conscious recently by the sinking of a United States merchant ship off Neah Bay just fifty-nine miles west of Victoria and by the landing of Japanese forces in the outer fringe of the Aleutian Islands far to the northwest." The page two headline declared: Japs' Shelling Held Harmless. Even Prime Minister Mackenzie King seemed more concerned about the fall of the north African fortress of Tobruk than about Estevan. On June 23 he commented: "It is as critical a situation in the Middle East as has arisen since the war commenced. And there have been other evidences in the past forty-eight hours that in this world-encircling conflict Canada is coming more and more into the zone of immediate danger."

Third, the war was going disastrously for the Allies in the early summer of 1942. Tobruk fell to General Irwin Rommel on the same day as the Estevan incident. Twenty-five thousand British soldiers were taken prisoner along with mountains of supplies—enough to keep the Afrika Korps plentifully supplied for almost a year. In Russia, the German steamroller was driving deep into the south. The huge fortress of Sebastopol in the Crimea fell on July 3, after a siege of 250 days—with a loss of more than 100,000 Russian soldiers and thousands of tanks and guns. The Don River was breached the next day, and on July 7, Voronezh surrendered. In the Atlantic, German U-boats were sinking vital convoy ships many times faster then they could be built. In 1942 alone, more than 1,500 ships with a gross tonnage of 6,226,215 were lost to submarines—while U-boat operational strength in the Atlantic surged from 91 to 212. Winston Churchill later wrote, "The U-boat attack of 1942 was our worst evil." In the Pacific, the Japanese occupied Attu, Kiska and Aggatu in the Aleutians by early June, and seemed poised to strike both Alaska and northern British Columbia. With all of this very genuine bad news, there was really no need for any Canadian or American government to stage a phony attack on Estevan.

An interesting question does remain. How does one explain the sightings of several vessels acting in concert off Estevan that night? For days after the shellings, the Allies combed the seas for a "surface raider" or two submarines, which were never found. The observers' stories varied—on the west coast, visibility at dusk in misty June is notoriously poor, and Robert Lally, a key witness, had no binoculars. Contrary to what was reported by both Donald Graham and "Fifth Estate," most of the eyewitnesses reported only a single submarine in the deepening dusk. According to Edward T. Redford, the experienced Officer in Charge, who had lost an arm in World War I:

The submarine surfaced about two miles off shore and was plainly visible. Shelling commenced at approximately 9:40 p.m. and con-tinued for about 40 minutes. The first shells landed on the beach about 100 yards [90 m] in front of the lighthouse. Mr. Lally, who was the lightkeeper at the time, immediately put out the light. The sub apparently then raised its sights, for from then on the shells went over-head…The submarine pulled out on the surface and everyone could see her and hear the diesel engines quite clearly. While naturally there was some nervousness, everyone, including women and children, took the whole incident in their stride, then spent the following day souvenir hunting.

Captain James L. Detwiler of HMCS *San Tomas* later interviewed a Native woman from Hesquiat. "She was sincere," he reported, "and tried to make me understand that she knew the difference between a whale and a boat. She said that she first thought it was a whale, but when it didn't splash or 'blow' she knew it was a boat." Mrs. Lally, wife of the lightkeeper, had this to say:

Canadian warships passed the lighthouse almost daily. I saw two early in the morning of the shelling, so the sound of gunfire that night didn't bother me. I thought it was target practice. I was just putting the youngest of the children to bed when the first shell exploded on the beach. "That's pretty poor shooting! It came pretty close," I yelled to my husband who had just come down from turning on the lighthouse for the night. "Get the hell out of here! It's a Jap sub and they are shelling the lighthouse!" my husband Mike shouted back. More shells sailed overhead.

All of the eyewitness accounts that night must be taken with a grain of salt. Visibility was just too poor, and the imagination can play strange tricks in times of stress—particularly when events are recalled years later. The spectacular light show produced by the submarine's 14-cm gun, as well as her large and noisy presence, may well have impaired the witnesses' ability to observe events coolly and objectively. Certainly there was a wide variety of conflicting accounts of that exciting evening.

The five submarine attacks on North America demonstrated the weaknesses as well as the strengths of the Imperial Navy's submarine service. Navigating those thousands of kilometres of trackless Pacific expanse for months at a time, launching and recovering float planes at night, and evading endless searches demanded courage, discipline and competence. Yet nothing of importance was accomplished. The attacks were too sporadic and too far apart to make much of an impression—and the marksmanship was abysmal. No doubt the Japanese were hopeful of creating the same kind of sensation that Doolittle's B-25 bombing raid had generated in Japan. But as the war deteriorated for the Japanese, their subs were called back to protect her navy in the home islands; by September 1942, they had left our Pacific coasts forever. Many ended up as supply vessels serving isolated island garrisons in the Pacific. The clear and shallow waters surrounding these islands provided little protection for large submarines. Most were soon lost, and the morale of the Imperial submarine service plummeted.

The night watch. Robert Lally was lightkeeper at Estevan Point the night of the shelling. (*photo by Robert Lally*)

The Japanese never learned to use their submarines as effectively as other countries during the war. The military also grossly underestimated the danger of Allied submarine fleets and paid a heavy price because of that error in judgement. Half of Japan's maritime tonnage lost was to submarines. American and German submariners sank anything that could carry a cargo, but the Japanese never developed the submarine "wolfpack" hunting technique essential for systematic destruction of the Allies' commerce fleet. After 1942, the huge volume of cargo vessels running between the mainland and the Pacific war zone was left almost untouched.

Instead, the Imperial Navy concentrated its strategic thinking on capital warships.

Japanese submarine commanders were given a strict priority list of what to attack—carriers first, battleships second, cruisers third, and so on. Merchant ships could only be targeted if there was no other warship in the area. There were even stipulations on how many torpedoes could be expended on each type of target. Fire everything if you faced a battleship, three at a cruiser and only one at a cargo vessel.

Bushido, the Samurai code of honour, may well have been a factor in these policies. Bushido taught that it was morally wrong to attack noncombatants randomly. War was fought between warriors who were expected never to surrender and to die for their cause if necessary. Blowing a helpless cargo carrier to kingdom come simply did not fit in with this code of ethics.

Interestingly, Bushido may have also played a role in the selection of west coast targets in 1942. After the war ended, Captain Ryonosuka Imamura, Secretary to the Japanese Naval Ministry, was asked why more populated targets had not been chosen. He replied, "You ask why we didn't shell some coastal United States city rather than Fort Stevens and [the] Santa Barbara oil tanks. At Santa Barbara it was our decision to shell oil tanks because we felt them important war assets. So it was with Fort Stevens. We didn't use these attacks to terrorize your people, but to strike war blows."

There can be little doubt that a Japanese submarine attacked the Estevan complex in June 1942. In his appearance on "Fifth Estate," Donald Graham argued convincingly that in wartime, governments manipulate and even create news for propaganda purposes. Two good examples are the phony Gulf of Tonkin incident in 1964, and stories of Iraqi soldiers removing Kuwaiti babies from maternity wards in 1990. But the theory that the Estevan shelling was nothing more than a setup cannot be supported by the evidence: physical traces, eyewitness accounts, submariners' stories and information on other Japanese military activities in the Pacific all contradict the theory.

And so does Canadian history. Graham's contention that the attack played a major role in the conscription

The lightstation circa 1950. Note that the wartime gray has been replaced with the striking white and bright red paint we see today.

debate is a weak one. The ambiguous results of the conscription plebiscite held on April 27, 1942 led Prime Minister Mackenzie King to waffle and delay any action for as long as possible. "Not necessarily conscription, but conscription if necessary" neatly defined (or obscured) the issue. Every Canadian male over age sixteen had to register for national service, but only volunteers were sent to the front. Not until 1944, when the Allies suffered heavy losses in Italy and France did King send the "Zombies" (the new recruits) to fight overseas.

Canadians today feel resentful and suspicious of our federal government. Who can blame them? Unemployment is alarmingly high in some regions, services are being cut back, national unity seems unachievable, the smell of corruption wafts through many official transactions. West coast lightkeepers themselves have never been treated with proper respect, and now the Canadian government has judged that many of their invaluable services can be replaced by machines and computers. But to extrapolate from state misdeeds that an act of war was staged by the government is to make a serious mistake.

No one can know every detail of what happened at Estevan Point on June 20, 1942. But the evidence shows that there was no political conspiracy: a Japanese submarine attacked Estevan, as well as four other sites on the west coast of North America during the spring and summer of 1942. ◆

Sources

Fujita, Nobuo and Joseph D. Harrington. "I bombed the U.S.A.," in US Naval Institute Proceedings, June 1961, pp. 64–69.

Graham, Donald. *Keepers of the Light*. Madeira Park, BC: Harbour Publishing, 1985.

New York Times, June 22, 1942, p. 9.

Toronto Globe and Mail, June 22, 1942, p. 1.

Victoria Daily Colonist, June 22, 1942, p. 5.

Victoria Daily Times, June 22, 1942, p. 1.

Webber, Bert. *Retaliation: Japanese Attacks and Allied Countermeasures on the Pacific Coast in World War II*, Corvallis: Oregon State University Press, 1975.

Webber, Bert. *Silent Siege III: Japanese Attacks on North America in World War II*. Medford, Oregon: Webb Research Group, 1997.

Light at the End of the World
Three Months on Cape St. James, 1941

by Hallvard Dahlie

In August 1786, the French explorer Comte de la Perouse sighted the southernmost tip of what is now the Queen Charlotte Islands and named it Cap Hector. The following year, Captain George Dixon saw it on St. James Day (July 25) and renamed it Cape St. James. He also named the island chain, the Queen Charlotte Islands, after his ship.

A lightstation was established on the cape in 1912–13, and for the next eighty years the island was occupied. It was an isolated outpost, and when the mission ship Thomas Crosby III *visited in 1926, the keeper's wife, Mrs. Lawrence, had not seen another woman for five years! The cape was, and is, one of the windiest spots on the BC coast: in 1985, the anemometer was pegged, recording gusts of over 190 km/hr.*

During the Second World War, just after this story takes place, the site served as one of a chain of early warning radar stations along the BC coast. From the summer of 1942 until the end of the war, up to seventy-five Air Force personnel at a time could be housed in a variety of buildings constructed on every flat bit of rock.

The station was turned over to the Meteorological Branch as a weather station in 1957, and in 1992, the light and weather station were automated and the cape was destaffed. Keeping with government policy, all structures were demolished.

—courtesy Jas. A.C. Derham-Reid, Meteorological Branch, Cape St. James, 1986–1992

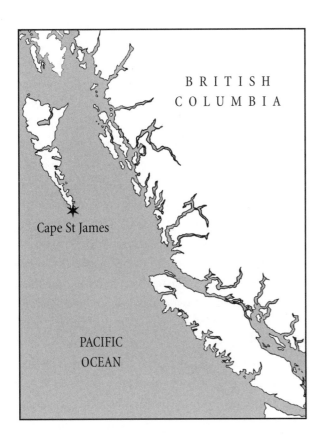

A strange interlude in my brief seafaring life took place in the fall of 1941, when I signed on as assistant lighthouse keeper at Cape St. James, a light perched on top of a three-hundred-foot rock at the very southern tip of the Queen Charlotte Islands. I had quit school earlier that year, at the age of sixteen, and found a job on the CGS *Alberni*, a lighthouse tender operating out of Prince Rupert. But when she had to go into drydock at the beginning of September for a new wartime grey paint job and a bit of refurbishing, I chose to take a stint out at the lighthouse rather than scrape barnacles and paint for three months.

From a trip to the Cape earlier that summer, I knew full well how bleak and totally isolated this place was, and as we crossed Hecate Strait to anchor in the deserted

An aerial view of Cape St. James, spring 1941, just before Hallvard Dahlie arrived for his three-month stint as assistant keeper.
(courtesy Jas. A.C. Derham-Reid)

whaling station of Jedway, I wondered what I had let myself in for. I remembered stories told by one of our deckhands about former keepers. One of them lived there with his companion, a gargantuan woman who hoarded all the food and released small amounts in exchange for sex, until finally starvation overcame his dwindling passion and he chased her out of the house with an axe. Then there was the story about the keeper who had gone mad one day and painted all the rooms in the house a bright marine red—walls and ceilings alike. These stories may have been exaggerated or fanciful, but they always reminded me of the lines from Gibson's "Flannan Isle," one of the few poems I had liked back in grade nine:

> And how the rock had been the death
> Of many a likely lad—
> How six had come to a sudden end
> And three had gone stark mad.

So, as the *Alberni* rounded the last headland of Kunghit Island the next morning, and I saw the tower looming out of the haze, my stomach sank as it came home to me that this is where I was to live, with a complete stranger, for the next three months or so. There was certainly no way to escape from it, for the high rock on which the tower and dwelling were perched was separated from Kunghit Island by a narrow strait. Here the waters of the Pacific and of Hecate Strait met in a steady, roaring maelstrom that must be impossible to cross, and in every other direction there was nothing but open sea.

The captain had assured me that the present keeper, a Newfoundlander by the name of Herb Fitzgerald, was a kind and gentle fellow. But what would I do, I wondered, as we rowed in toward the landing, if he should suddenly go mad? Or if he was a bit fruity, like the chief steward I had worked under for a while on the *Alberni*?

I had seen the keeper briefly on that earlier trip as he checked over the supplies we were unloading from the workboat, but I hadn't talked to him or looked all that closely at him. What I did remember was that he talked all the time, not to anyone in particular, but just talked, as though he had stored up a horde of words for a long time, and now had a chance to release them. As we rowed back to the *Alberni*, my rowing mate had said, "Look at that poor bugger, going back up to that tower all by himself." There he was, climbing slowly up the long tramway, stooped over and limping a bit, steadying himself by holding on to the steel cable, and never once turning to look back at us, as though seeing us depart would confirm something he didn't want to acknowledge.

And now he was busy loading supplies onto the tram car as I stood apart from him at the end of the jetty, watching my mates row back to the *Alberni*. The workboat rose high on the crest of a towering wave that had banked off the rocks, then disappeared into a deep trough, with only the head, shoulders and arms of Second Mate MacKay visible as he stood in the stern controlling the steering oar. "Ye'll be all right," he had comforted me in his soft Scottish burr as they prepared to shove off. "I've known old Herb here for some while now, and he's a right decent fellow. He'll do nothing to harm you, and we'll be back to pick you up in early December." With that, I was struck by the full realization of my abandonment. I waved frantically as the workboat reappeared on the next crest, but no one noticed me, and the boat disappeared around the rock bluff.

All this time I had been vaguely aware of a chattering going on behind me, and now Herb's voice came more clearly. "We'd better get a move on and get these supplies up, for it could be storming soon," he was saying, straightening up from belaying a support rope around the cleats of the loaded tram car. "The glass was falling when I left the house, and storms come up awfully fast around here. We'll come down later for the two fuel drums and the sacks of coal, but I don't want our food to get wet."

He had come down from the dwelling just as we arrived at the jetty, and when MacKay introduced me, he looked surprised, as though he were expecting an older person. He was a tall, thin, grey-haired man with a slight stoop and a mouth that looked as though it was always grinning—which disconcerted me at first, for I thought he was always laughing at me, even when he was talking, which was most of the time.

"I didn't know you were coming today," he had explained, rattling on to MacKay, "and I was sound asleep when your damn whistle woke me up. I was up all bloody night running the foghorn as well as tending the light, and I didn't sleep hardly at all, so when there was no fog at daylight when I put out the light I thought I might as well sleep for a while because it isn't that often I can sleep that long around here, and then that damn whistle woke me up and by the time I started the gas engine and got the tram car down you guys were damn

Sixteen-year-old Hallvard Dahlie at Prince Rupert in 1941. "I chose to take a stint out at the lighthouse rather than scrape barnacles and paint for three months."

near in to the jetty already," and he went on and on, just barely stopping when MacKay told him I was to join him for the next three months.

And though he was puffing heavily as we walked up the long tramway, he kept talking all the way up, even when we stopped to rest so he could catch his breath. In fact, that first day he stopped only when he fell asleep. Even then I thought I heard some sounds coming from his room upstairs, but perhaps it was only the first of many strange noises I was to hear in that house. His sharp blue eyes pierced into mine as he spoke, as though he was afraid I might try to escape; fascinated by him and somewhat afraid, I don't think I said more than a dozen words to him that first day. I remembered parts of Coleridge's poem, for it intrigued me in much the same way that "Flannan Isle" did, and like the Ancient Mariner, old Herb held me "with his glittering eye" and I could not "choose but hear," for there was no escape.

There were, however, a number of specific tasks to learn and to do that first day, and here Herb was efficiency itself, wasting not a word or a motion. He showed me how to start the gas engine in the shed on top of the tramway and how to release and rewind the cable, so we spent a couple of hours hauling up the fuel drums, sacks of coal and remaining supplies. He demonstrated the operation of the foghorn, and most exciting to me, he showed me how to operate the light itself, situated in the concrete tower about a hundred and fifty feet beyond the house, at the very highest point of our rocky island.

"There are two things you must never allow to happen at a lighthouse," he told me as we headed for the tower. "Never let the light burn during daylight hours, and never let the light stop revolving during darkness, for both of these are signals of distress. Any ship that observes these conditions has to come in and check or radio someone for help, for they mean an emergency of sorts at the light." He pulled open the heavy metal door and motioned me in ahead of him. "And if it isn't an emergency, but just a case of our own carelessness, we really catch hell from the Department of Transport. I heard of a keeper down at one of the southern lights who got fired for being careless twice, so we can't afford to make any mistakes."

The ground level area of the tower was dark and

Bleak and remote, Cape St. James light is perched on top of a three-hundred-foot rock. The lightkeeper's house is to the left of the light. Note the tramway and boat landing. (*courtesy Jas. A.C. Derham-Reid*)

cold and damp, and in its hollowness Herb's voice ricocheted off the concrete walls as we climbed the steel steps to the next level. "This is what they call the Fresnel system," he explained as he went up ahead of me, "and up here on the second level is where we keep the fuel tanks and winding mechanism. I'll show you how to operate these in a minute, but let's go up to the top level first, where I'll explain the light itself and the kind of work we have to do during the day."

We climbed the second set of steel stairs, and I was dazzled by the sudden light as I reached the upper level. For here there was nothing but glass—huge curved panels around the circumference of the tower top and massive prisms enclosing the light itself, and the late afternoon sun bathed everything in a brilliant translucence. Herb explained how the prisms gather the light produced by the mantles and concentrate it into a strong ray that passes through the central eye of the prisms, producing the powerful beam that revolves at a certain speed. "Every light on the coast revolves at a different speed," he continued, "so if a captain has to check his position, and can get a glimpse of a light, he can check his directory of lights and figure out where he is. That's why it's so important for us to keep these prisms absolutely clean, and all this surrounding glass, too, on both the inside and outside," and he opened a hinged glass panel so we could step out onto the surrounding catwalk.

"It's not bad out here when it's fairly calm, like today," he said, grabbing the handrail and staring out over the sea, "but sometimes the damn wind almost blows you off as you're washing these panels, so you have to be careful. Believe it or not, in the big storms we get out here, I've seen the spray from the waves blow right up and drench these windows."

I looked down at the ocean, four hundred feet straight below the west side of the tower, and even on this relatively windless day, could see the billowing waves washing high up the side of the cliffs. I scanned the sea in all directions and far off to the west thought I saw a smudge of smoke. But I couldn't be sure; it could have been a cloud or just a mirage. There was nothing else in any direction, and I realized that if we did run into any trouble out here, it could be ages before any help arrived. Off the south shore of our island was a narrow spit of rocks jutting into the sea, on which I saw movement.

"Them's sea lions," Herb explained, following my gaze. "There's thousands of them, it seems, and you should hear the noise they make if something disturbs them. You'd think it was a bunch of babies howling, and in the middle of the night it can really give you a fright.

But let's go back in, and I'll show you how to light the lamp and keep it revolving."

The lamp mechanism was really quite simple, consisting of two rather large mantles, much like the kind we had on our gas lamps back on the homestead, but it was fuelled by kerosene rather than gas, kept in tanks on the second level. Beside the tanks was a drum with a winding mechanism and a thin wire cable wound tightly around it, whose end was attached to a heavy weight. "As soon as you light the lamp," Herb explained carefully, "you have to come straight down here and release this catch so that the weight starts slowly unwinding the cable, which revolves the drum, which in turn through this set of gears rotates the light." All that seemed pretty clear, but Herb went through the whole process again, so I paid close attention, thinking of his earlier warning about carelessness. "And we have to be sure to get up here every two hours to rewind the drum and pump up the pressure in these tanks, otherwise everything will come to a stop. I'll come up with you tonight and watch you light the lamp, and make sure you do everything the right way, but after tonight you're on your own, okay?"

So that's how our routine was set up: I was to take the first shift, from six to midnight, then I would wake Herb and go to bed. Herb would extinguish the light at daybreak, and if there wasn't any fog, he would go to bed for a couple of hours. Then we'd have our breakfast and go about our routines of the day.

It was a ridiculously large house that the two of us occupied, built perhaps in the expectation that lightkeepers would sire many children, but the only large family I saw that summer was over at Triple Island, and that seemed to be the exception. Here there were some thirteen rooms on two floors, a half basement, and a large covered verandah along the south wall where the main entrance was. The front room had two large windows looking out on this porch and a smaller window on the west wall, through which we could see the tower. The kitchen had one large window looking out to the east and north, and as I waited for Herb to come down for breakfast each morning, I would sit at the kitchen table looking out this window and scanning the coast along the east side of Kunghit Island for any sign of a ship, though I knew that the *Alberni* wouldn't be along until early December.

"See anything yet, laddie?" were always the first words Herb said, his mouth turned up into more of a grin than usual, and he repeated these words every day that I was there, though as we got closer to December, I thought his grin seemed less pronounced. He was always partially dressed when he came downstairs, carrying his checkered lumberjack shirt, his heavy black trousers held up over his winter underwear by a pair of bright red suspenders. He would yawn as he peered out the window for a moment, brushing back his thinning grey hair with quick strokes of his hand, then disappear into a small washroom off the back of the kitchen, where we stored our barrel of rainwater for washing and cooking.

The house had no plumbing of any sort, and we took baths in the same galvanized washtub we used for our laundry, rare as either of these activities was. I can't remember Herb ever washing his black trousers—by the end of my stay I'm sure they could stand by themselves—and I wasn't much better. My bed had two sheets and a pillowcase and I would reverse top and bottom sheets, then turn them over and repeat the routine, turn my pillow over when one side got unbearably dirty, then turn it inside out and repeat that routine. All this was done before any washing, and I felt pretty proud of my ingenuity.

And we had a precarious outhouse, the likes of which I had seen only once before, set at the very edge of a cliff beside a prospector's shack up in the mountains above my home town in the interior of BC. But because of the constant winds at Cape St. James, this one seemed even more risky. It was perched on the edge of a ravine a hundred feet or so from our back door and anchored with heavy cables to four concrete-embedded eye bolts. We could look through the hole straight down a couple of hundred feet to where the ravine angled out sharply to a rock outcropping. Sitting there as the roaring winds shook and buffeted this structure was an absolute assurance against constipation.

Off the west wall of the kitchen was a small cubbyhole, sort of like a pantry, with a chair and a small counter that served as a desk. Because we had only a coal oil lamp for light, it was in that room where we passed the long hours of the night, reading whatever we found in some boxes of old books and magazines an earlier keeper had left behind. This room had one long, narrow window whose blind I always pulled down at night, because it was sort of scary to see my reflection looking back at me from outside, the glass distorting my face and head as though my hair was standing straight up.

With the wind almost always howling, the house itself creaked and groaned, with noises seeming to come from all thirteen rooms, or from somewhere outside. I would step out of the cubbyhole into the darkness of the kitchen, hardly breathing, my heart pumping furiously, as I tried to assure myself that there was nothing to be afraid of. But what were those footsteps? Was it old Herb walking about directly over my head? No, his room was at the other end of the house, so I thought about the keeper with the axe, and the madman who painted the rooms red, and I thought of "Flannan Isle" and wondered, was I going mad, too? Then the noises died away and I tiptoed back into my little well-lit room, trying to find comfort in the pile of magazines I had already thumbed through countless times, magazines like *Liberty*, *Mechanics Illustrated* and a 1938 issue of *Life* that showed Chamberlain returning from Munich and what I kept turning back to, an exposé of a Greenwich Village artist's model in various stages of undress.

Then my blood froze, for I heard someone out on the front porch, knocking on the window—or rather, sort of scratching on the windowpanes. I thought stupidly, why don't they knock on the door? I moved silently to my little doorway, the lamp behind me throwing an enormous shadow on the kitchen wall, then I tiptoed cautiously and nervously to the door that led into the front room, from where I could look out the windows to the porch. I yelled in unmitigated panic, for there, up against the window, all dressed in white, was a figure waving its arms and bouncing up and down, as though trying to find a way to get in. I could see him—or it— because the lantern we carried to the tower stood lighted on the porch, but I didn't think I could be seen, for I was in darkness, and that gave me some courage. Then something else took over in my mind and said, there can't be anyone out there, we're on an isolated rock hundreds of miles from any settlement, so where would anybody come from? And old Herb is sound asleep upstairs. And then I said to myself, of course, old Herb, and that white figure out on the porch immediately and with a stomach-filling relief transformed itself into Herb's winter underwear that he had washed that afternoon and hung on the line to dry, now frozen stiff by the icy winds.

It took me some time to work up enough nerve to go out to the porch for the lantern and make my way up to the dark tower and tend the light, a scary enough task without all this extra fear.

That was probably the longest night I spent in that house, and when I woke Herb, he said, "Did I hear someone yell during the night, or was I dreaming again? I have the damnedest dreams about this place." I told him he must have been dreaming, but he looked at me in a funny way, his grin more enigmatic than usual.

In that little cubbyhole, too, we kept our battery-operated radio on which, every morning at nine o'clock

"I yelled in unmitigated panic, for there, up against the window, all dressed in white, was a figure waving its arms and bouncing up and down, as though trying to find a way to get in." *(illustration by Alistair Anderson)*

sharp, we received our daily instructions from the Department of Transport office in Victoria. These instructions were always read by the same person, whom I visualized as a rather frail old man, dressed in tweeds, with a pointed beard and thin lips that barely opened as he read, for the message would come through in a somewhat pinched and shaky tone: "Attention all lightkeepers on the Pacific Coast. Here are your instructions for today. Carry out instructions 'A for Apple.' I repeat, to all lightkeepers on the Pacific Coast, carry out instructions 'A for Apple.' This is the end of today's message."

There would be a bit of crackling static as the gentleman turned off the microphone, and we would immediately shut off the radio, for we knew that the C battery would not last forever and Herb always liked to listen to the six o'clock news before going to bed.

"A for Apple," Herb told me, meant that we were to carry out normal operations for the light and foghorn, and these instructions didn't change the whole time I was there. "If you ever hear instructions 'B for Butter'," he explained, "that means that an enemy is approaching the coast in ships or submarines, and then we can't have the light or any signals operating." That sounded far more exciting to me, but it never happened while I was there. But as things turned out, if I had stayed one day longer, then 'B for Butter' would have been the order of the day, for the *Alberni* came to pick me up the day before Pearl Harbor.

To be more accurate, I should have said that the "A for Apple" message came not for as long as I was there, but as long as the radio's C battery lasted, and I remember precisely the day it died for it was largely my fault. I had always been a baseball fan and it hadn't been that long since my hero, Johnny van der Meer, had pitched two no-hit games in a row for the Cincinnati Reds. Now here it was October, World Series time.

So, in spite of Herb's injunction to keep the radio off except for the news, I would surreptitiously turn it on after he had gone to bed, with the volume on low, to hear as much of the Yankees–Dodgers series as I could. I heard parts of games two and three, but the weakening battery had made each broadcast increasingly faint.

Then, on the fifth day of October, I was listening to game four with my ear pressed hard against the speaker, and it was two out in the ninth for the Yankees, with Brooklyn leading four to three. "It's a swing and a miss for strike three!" I barely heard the announcer say, and then his voice rose in excitement, helping to compensate for the dying battery. "The catcher dropped the ball! Mickey Owen dropped the ball, and Heinrich is running to—" And that is all I heard, for at that moment the battery went absolutely dead, and no amount of coaxing could bring it back to life. I had no idea, until the *Alberni* came two months later, what had happened in the rest of that game or who won the World Series.

The days went by very quickly at first as the novelty of the place kept me intrigued, then more slowly as I waited for the *Alberni* to return. For Herb, all the days must have gone by too quickly. That first evening we had reached a unanimous decision, on the evidence of the meal Herb had prepared, that I would be cook, and his spirits had lifted visibly. "I'm so damn fed up with macaroni and canned tomatoes," he complained, as I looked with some misgivings at the gooey red and white mixture on my plate, "that it won't matter what you prepare, it's bound to be an improvement."

We had countless cans of powdered milk and I was good at making porridge, so that was our breakfast every morning, along with bread and jam and strong coffee. Herb had ordered generous quantities of chops, cutlets, ham steaks and other meat cuts that we stored in the basement, so our dinners didn't stray much from the meat and potatoes variety, which suited both of us. Dessert was no problem, for Herb had ordered two or three cases of his favourite, canned pineapple, but one rainy day I thought I would surprise him with a change—I cooked a rice and raisin pudding. What I hadn't realized was how uncontrollably rice would multiply when cooked, so for a few days we had to forgo the pineapple. I baked bread on two or three occasions, and once I made a batch of oatmeal cookies that not even the dampness of the whole Pacific Ocean could prevent from setting like concrete.

Our other tasks we organized according to the weather, and on the few fine days we had, we spent much of the time gathering firewood, for we had to use our coal sparingly. We picked up pieces of driftwood along the rocky shoreline, hauled them up on the tram car, then cut them into suitable pieces with a Swede saw and axe and stored them in the lean-to off the kitchen. The tide and wind normally brought in a large supply of driftwood every day, but once after a horrendous storm that lasted an entire day and night, we searched in vain. Every stick of wood, and even huge logs that had been wedged behind rocks far up the steep slopes, had been dislodged and carried out to sea.

When we felt we needed a break from this heavy work, we launched Herb's small clinker-built rowboat to try our luck at fishing. Herb would deftly manipulate the boat into suitable spots and I would jig off the stern and usually catch one or two rock cod or red snapper. On one of these fishing trips, a whale surfaced close to our boat, then dived toward us and came up directly underneath us, lifting our small boat almost clear of the water. If Herb had not moved quickly to wallop it with his oar, we would certainly have capsized, and the whale's wide tail flapped dangerously close to us as it shot away like a giant silvery dark arrow toward the swirling current of the narrow strait.

We were always careful in these dangerous waters to stay close to our shore, but one day the sea was unusually calm so we rowed across the strait to Kunghit Island and pulled our boat up on its sandy shore. All around us we found green glass balls, transparent and beautiful, ranging from baseball size to something two or three times the size of a basketball. "These are Japanese fishing floats," Herb explained, "broken free from their nets somewhere out there," and he pointed his thumb toward the west. I wondered if they had floated all the way from Japan, or if they were harbingers of something closer to our shores. But like intruders coming upon some secret cache of treasures, we left them where we found them and headed back to our own island against a stiffening wind.

And one warm, windless Sunday afternoon we were up on the catwalk cleaning the windows of the tower, with Herb talking as much as ever, when over his voice I heard the sound of something else, like an engine, get-

ting louder very quickly—and suddenly we ducked. For coming straight at us from the north, and only fifty feet or so above the tower, was a seaplane, dipping its wings in some kind of crazy salute. It dived down the south side of the island, sending hundreds of squealing, terrified sea lions off the rocks, and then it circled out to sea and came back for a landing in toward our jetty. We had seen the pilot waving at us as he roared past, and we saw the RCAF insignia on the wings and body, so we assumed it was from the air base at Alliford Bay, up at the north end of Moresby Island.

I was quite excited about seeing someone else after all this time, and we hurried down off the tower to go to meet them. My imagination ran wild: Japanese fishing floats, radio going dead—had something happened that we didn't know about? Or were they coming to get me, or perhaps they had a message from my family, for I hadn't seen my mother before I came out here, but had only left a note on the kitchen table: "Have gone out to Cape St. James for three months. Will be back in early December. Don't worry." As we waited at the top of the tramway for them to appear, Herb told me about a German fellow who was a keeper over at Ivory Island during the first war, and who was fired for being a security threat. "Maybe they think you're German instead of Norwegian," he joked, "and they're coming out to check on you!"

But it wasn't nearly that dramatic. The crew was simply out on a routine patrol, had seen us up on the tower and decided on the spur of the moment to drop in on us and present us with a fresh salmon they had caught earlier that day on the west coast of Moresby. They stayed for a half hour or so, had some coffee and a couple of my concrete cookies, then took off up the east coast of Kunghit Island, leaving us to silence and ourselves. It was a welcome visit nevertheless, reminding us that we weren't totally forgotten by the rest of the world after all.

But that Sunday was the last warm day of the fall, and the gloomy days passed slowly after that. The steady rain and wind kept us indoors most of the time, and the decreasing visibility made me feel more trapped and isolated than ever. Herb tried to lift my spirits one afternoon

The light tower at Cape St. James, circa 1957. *(courtesy Jas. A.C. Derham-Reid)*

by giving me a haircut, but he was unpractised and the scissors were dull, so what resulted was a straight line across the back of my head, a series of jagged steps up each side, just missing my ears, then a straight cut across the front that made me look like Ella Cinders. "Will you do mine now?" he asked when he had finished, and I said, "Sure, how do you want it cut?" and he said, "Off." So that's what I did, and for the next little while I don't think either one of us looked in the mirror much.

One morning in early December, Herb slept in longer than usual. I had finished eating my porridge and put the lid back on the pot to keep his warm, and was on my second cup of coffee before he came down. For once he didn't look out the window or say "See anything yet, laddie?" but went straight to the washroom. It was a gloomy morning, with clouds hanging low over Kunghit Island, and I had seen nothing in the hour or so I had been waiting for him. But when he came out of the washroom, cleanly shaven and washed, and dressed in his black trousers and checkered shirt, he said, "Well, today's the day. I feel it in my bones, and besides, I had a dream last night about a ship running aground on those rocks where all the sea lions are, so that must mean something. Maybe they need you back as quartermaster to steer the damn thing!" His grin lit up his face momentarily as he sat down and vigorously stirred his coffee, but his actions all seemed forced that morning. As I cleaned up the kitchen, he sat at the table, slumped over, just staring out the window, seemingly at nothing.

Sure enough, his bones were right. Just before lunch I detected a grey shape coming around the headland of Kunghit Island, barely visible through the haze and rain. It was still too far away to determine whether it was the *Alberni*, and I didn't want to get my hopes up too soon, so I didn't look out again until I had prepared lunch and put it on the table. When I looked again there was no doubt, even though she was now all grey from stem to stern, where before her superstructure had been white and yellow. If nothing else, the huge balloon of black smoke from her funnel gave her away, for only coal-

burners produced such a volume of smoke, and the *Alberni* hadn't yet converted to oil.

I was excited at the prospect of rejoining the crew, but I didn't know what I should say to Herb, who scarcely touched his lunch, saying he wasn't very hungry because he had had a late breakfast. He got up quickly from the table, grabbed his rain slicker and said, without looking at me, "I'd better go out and start the gas engine. You'd better pack your things to send down on the tram car, because they'll be rowing in within the hour."

He knew full well that I didn't have much to pack, only a duffel bag full of dirty clothes, but I knew he wanted to be alone for a while, so I packed slowly, folding each garment carefully, then stripped the bed and swept out my room. I put the two sheets and the pillowcase in a tub of cold rain water in the washroom, where only a miracle soap could ever make them white again. Then I stood in the kitchen and took a last look around, a bit smug, I suppose, over the fact that I had come through these last three months quite unchanged, except for my haircut.

But I couldn't forget how I sat terrified in that little cubbyhole off the kitchen night after night, so afraid at the thought of having to walk up to that dark tower, flickering lantern in hand, not knowing what I might meet behind that heavy door. And then climbing the clanging steps up to the second level to pump up the tank and wind the weight mechanism, lifting the lantern above me to place it on the landing before I stuck my head up, in case there was something there. I remembered how one night, not long after Herb's underwear almost incapacitated me, the long blind on the tall, narrow window suddenly shot up without warning and I leaped out of my chair, paralyzed with fear, seeing my white face in the window staring back at me. No, there were things about Cape St. James lighthouse that I would not miss, and roused out of my memories by a loud, prolonged blast of the *Alberni*'s whistle, I put on my rain gear, grabbed my duffel bag, and went out to join Herb. ◆

Claus Carl Daniel Botel
West Coast Patriarch

by Ruth Botel

Claus Botel was born in 1868 in Schleswig/Holstein, located near the Danish border in northern Germany. He was a farmer like his father before him, and he and his wife raised a large family on a farm with horses, dairy cows and a generous kitchen garden. The income from the farm was not sufficient to support the household and Claus supplemented the farm income by working with his horse and wagon to fill in the approaches of the new railway bridge over the Keil Canal, and by catching poisonous snakes in the fields.

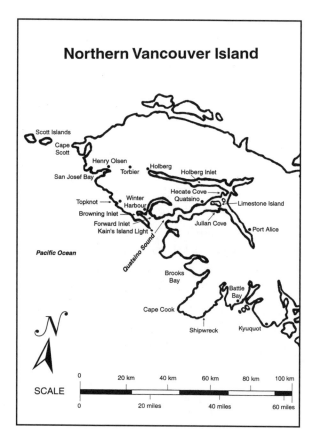

He pinned the snakes down with a long forked stick, then kept them in a sack or bottle and sold them to the local pharmacist or chemist, who used the venom for medicinal purposes. The family had a large, comfortable home with a slate roof, brick walls and oak beams. They owned the farm and had no debts.

But times were bleak in Germany in the years preceding World War One, and it became harder and harder to make a living. Claus was very worried about the future. He had seen a number of glowing advertisements about Canada in the newspapers—ads placed by the Canadian government, which was encouraging Europeans to come to this land of milk and honey. The advertisements told of generous grants of free land to those who came and settled. There were opportunities unlimited and jobs galore. In addition, the Canadian Pacific Railway promised free freight and transportation, once they were in Canada, to the nearest point of call to the family's grant. Claus's father and brother had already moved to North America.

Claus Botel studied maps of Canada and decided to look for a homestead in British Columbia, on Canada's west coast. He sold the farm and made the necessary arrangements. On April 9, 1913, the family—consisting of Claus, six children from his first marriage (the three older ones were out on their own), his wife Martha, her two children and their one-year-old son Gustav—departed from the port of Hamburg, Germany on the ship the *President Lincoln*. Martha was eight months pregnant. Besides paying for his own entourage of two adults and nine children, Claus paid another couple's way to Canada. (They repaid the money forty years later.) The journey to Canada took eleven days. They landed in Halifax on April 20, 1913.

After the lengthy procedure of going through customs and medical checks, the family boarded a train which would take them through the United States, then up to Vancouver. The plan was to visit briefly with Claus's father Hans, and his brother and wife, John and Marie, in Omaha, Nebraska.

On April 27, as Claus and Martha rode the train through the Wenatchee Valley in Washington, their baby was born in the passenger car, on one of the hard wooden seats. Claus assisted his wife, whose long voluminous skirts gave her the only privacy to be had during the birth. The family arrived in Vancouver, BC on April 29 and stayed overnight. The next day they headed for Victoria to apply for a homestead.

At the parliament buildings, someone was found to interpret for the Botel family, and a pre-emption of 160 acres was selected for them. They were told that this parcel of land was situated in a nice protected bay on the beautiful west coast of Vancouver Island, not far from Quatsino Sound. Here, they were informed, they could start a farm. A railway would be built nearby in the not too distant future, making it easier to get their supplies in and the produce out. In the meantime they could ship their produce out by boat. The family was enthusiastic about the parcel of land, eager to find it and get settled.

Sixteen-year-old John, the oldest of the children, decided to stay in Victoria and look for employment. They said their goodbyes and the rest of the Botel family boarded the 165-foot CPR boat the SS *Tees*.

The journey up the west coast of the island lasted five days. They put into little settlements along the way, dropping off passengers and freight. Finally they reached Quatsino Sound, then proceeded up the sound to the Botels' dropping-off point, the small wharf at Quiet Cove on Drake Island (then called Limestone Island). As the large family left the boat, having no idea where their homestead was or how to get there, the captain's parting words were: "You're on your own now."

Claus managed to find someone who understood and spoke German, and he arranged for a man named Sorenson to load his family and their belongings onto

Claus Botel with daughter Johanna in 1925.

his boat and take them to Holberg. It was late at night when they arrived at the dock, so the Botels—including Martha and the newborn Wenatchee—bedded down on the rough, cold floor of the freight shed.

The next morning, the family started on their long hike to San Josef Bay and the west coast of the island, where they understood they would find their homestead. The family consisted of Claus, aged forty-five; Martha, thirty; Anna, fourteen; Helene, eleven; Max, nine; Emma, seven; Willy, five; Willi Hecht, seven; Erna Hecht, four; Claus Jr., one; and baby Wenatchee, a week and a half old. The older ones helped the little ones along the trail bordered by alders, high salmonberry bushes and thick salal. They carried all their worldly possessions, including two feather mattresses and a pretty set of china dinnerware.

They reached Torbier's, just below Ronning's, the first day. Mr. Torbier spoke German. The family was exhausted and slept well that night. Up early the next day, they resumed their trek. They reached the mouth of the San Josef River and looked out on a long, wide bay of sparkling water bordered by white sandy beaches stretching out on both sides. Beyond this vista they could see the distant Pacific Ocean. They paused here to drink in the welcome sight, mother and father resting briefly while the children laughed and played and raced about making tracks in the sand.

It was suppertime when the exhausted group reached Henry Ohlsen's homestead, which included the store and post office of the small, remote community of San Josef. Claus and Martha were thankful to have found another family who understood German. The Ohlsen family prepared supper for the Botels and made a corner of their barn comfortable for them to spend the night.

The next morning, Henry Ohlsen and Claus went to seek out the Botel family's homestead, and found the land, fronted by sandy beach, about ten miles south down the rugged coast. Two weeks later the family set out, cutting their own trail through the evergreens of the Pacific rainforest and the extremely dense mossy underbrush and salal.

The pre-emption was at Top Knot—no neighbours for miles. There was some protection from the north and east winds but absolutely none from the south and west. The Botels had the unceasing roar of the ocean surf literally in their front yard, and during storms the noise was deafening.

Immediately the family commenced clearing. At first they had a tent, but it was blown away during a strong southwester a few days after their arrival. Next they built a drafty home from driftwood and weathered planks they found on the beach. Long shakes were made for the walls of the one-room cabin, short shakes for the roof. That first home blew over in a strong wind so they built another. This one had stronger supports, and it was farther up the beach where a sandbank and some tall evergreens gave better protection from the strong winds.

The garden was another priority. Potatoes and turnips were planted as land was cleared and soil was prepared. Come harvest time, these vegetables were excellent. The potato crop was bountiful, the other veg-

etables large and solid. When the turnips were cut open, the syrup literally dripped out.

Clearing the monster spruce and hemlock trees, some of them six to seven feet in diameter, was a mammoth undertaking. To remove some of them, Claus dug down under the main roots, cleared spaces and lit fires there as well as around the base of the tree. The children were kept busy feeding these fires. Sometimes it took up to two weeks of constant burning to bring a tree down. When the tree was finally down, Claus took his little bow saw, brought from Germany, and sawed the limbs into usable lengths. The new bucking saw was used on the massive trunk. With the hammer and the back of the axe, wooden wedges were driven into the sawed-up lengths to split them into manageable pieces, which the children stacked. All this activity gave the Botels a good supply of fuel for cooking, keeping warm and clearing the next trees.

When the family was somewhat settled in, Claus took two of the children, Max and Helene, with him and went to the Ohlsen homestead in hopes of purchasing a cow and calf. Henry Ohlsen was away, but his mother sold the Botels a Holstein cow named Bessy, a yearling steer and a calf. Bessy was young Violet Ohlsen's cow and Violet cried when the Botels took her away. As it turned out, Bessy did not live long. The trail which Claus and the boys had hacked out of the wilderness was crude— too crude for the animals. The cow and the steer each broke a leg and were butchered on the spot. The little heifer was packed back to the homestead on Claus's shoulders. He and his children made trips back and forth to pack home the meat, which was eventually salted down and stored.

Later Claus made another trip and bought a bull and a calf. This time it took a month to get the animals home—as they made their way along the trail, Claus and the children cut out every large root and windfall, making the path safe for the animals.

By the end of that first summer, the family knew they needed to have a boat. Claus took Max and Helene with him and went to buy a boat he had heard was for sale. He took the last of their money from the sale of the property in Germany. The three of them walked the twenty miles through the bush to Holberg, borrowed a skiff and rowed from Holberg to Winter Harbour, a distance of 50 miles. There, Claus bought a twenty-six-foot, round-bottomed cannery skiff. He transferred to it the sack of flour they'd bought at Holberg, a small sail, their meagre remaining supplies and his old gun (a relic from his term of service in the German forces). The winds were strong when they were ready to depart from Winter Harbour. They got as far as the lagoon in Browning Creek, then stopped at a little old shack on the point of the southwest side to wait for better weather. It was almost two weeks before they could make the journey home. While they waited, Claus and the kids trekked through the lagoon's marshes every day, often scaring up ducks and geese. Claus tried to bag a few of the birds without any success.

Finally a favourable day dawned and the eager trio set out for home. They hoped to be able to use the sail some of the time and give their arms a rest from rowing, although none of them had ever sailed before. They travelled down Browning Inlet and out Forward Inlet to Kains Island. Passing Kains Island, they found themselves on the rolling swells of the open Pacific Ocean, with no islands or bays for protection.

As they headed north toward home, a strong north wind came up and quickly built in intensity. The seas heaved higher and higher as the wind rose, and gallons of spray were whipped off the crests and splashed into the boat. As the weather deteriorated, the children bailed constantly while their father did his best to keep them afloat. The wind blew them far out to sea and eventually they lost sight of land. The storm continued

This photo, taken at the Botel's original homestead at Top Knot in the 1940s, shows Claus Botel's stepson, Willi Hecht, at his trapline cabin built with remnants of the original homestead building. Note the pole braces used to support the cabin in big blows.

the rest of the day. They had no idea where they were or in what direction lay the land. The exhausted children bailed all night long.

Finally, toward morning, the wind subsided. Claus still had no idea in which direction to row and the sail had blown away hours ago. All three were soaked, frightened, exhausted and cold. They took turns rowing just to keep warm. Claus waited for daybreak and then, knowing that the sun came up from where the land lay, they headed in that direction. It was evening when they stumbled ashore, happy to feel land under their feet.

They had no idea where they were as they climbed up the rocky shore. The children, in their excitement, forgot their fatigue. Once they got their land legs, they ran here and there scouting the bushline. Just as it was

Raccoons and a cougar skin are part of the bounty from Willi's trapline, circa 1945.

getting dark, they found an old cabin, belonging to Natives from Kyuquot. Inside, on the dirt floor, the exhausted father and children gave silent thanks that they were still alive, curled up together for warmth and fell into a heavy sleep.

While they slept, southeast gales came up, building a mountainous sea. At high tide the powerful storm grabbed the Botel's little skiff and destroyed it completely on the rocks. Luckily they had removed the damp bag of flour and their old axe, but the gun and the ammunition, left in the boat, were gone.

Day dawned and three hearts sank when they saw the scattered wreckage of the boat. Still, refreshed from their much-needed sleep, they began to explore their surroundings. It wasn't long before they spotted a small shake shack at the edge of the bush. It was a Shelter Shed, one of several sheds erected by the federal government in strategic places along the coast, to provide shelter for shipwrecked sailors. Each shed was stocked with

maps, charts and information in several languages. They learned that they were approximately forty miles from Top Knot, and in the lee of Cape Cook. The instructions said that an able-bodied man could walk to Quatsino in twenty-four hours.

The bedraggled, hungry trio packed up a small tent they found in the shed and set off at a fast pace. For two days they trekked the shoreline, stopping to rest by creeks, drinking their fill and then pressing on. As night fell they pitched the tent under the trees and curled up, watching the beam of light from Kains Island lighthouse. In the middle of the second night, a gale came up and tore the tent away, sending it up into the bushes farther along the beach and ripping it badly. Claus assessed their situation the next morning. After two days of walking they had only made it around the cape and could see into Brooks Bay. It seemed hopeless to go on. Disappointed, their enthusiasm gone, they headed back toward the Shelter Shed. On the way, they found their gun washed up on the beach. They picked it up and carried it with them, although it was of little use without ammunition.

What thoughts must have gone through Claus's mind as he trudged over the rocks and sand with his ten- and twelve-year-old children? They'd been away three weeks now. How were his wife Martha and fifteen-year-old Anna managing with the six young children? Was there enough food? Had they begun to fear the worst. Claus's thoughts must certainly have turned to the comfortable home and farm he had left in Germany. Money had been scarce, but there wasn't a shortage of food, the land was cleared and everyone spoke his language.

Back at the Shelter Shed, they read the list of instructions again and learned that if stranded people kept three fires going on the beach, any passing ship would be alerted to send in a boat to investigate and to pick them up. Luckily Claus had a few dry matches in a water-tight brass container which he always carried in his pocket. He, Max and Helene lit the three fires and kept them burning for quite a few days. Keeping the fires stoked must have kept the three of them busy and warm as they ran about hunting for wood and throwing it on the burning piles. Twice during this time they saw the lights of passing ships, but no boat came in.

As the days went by, food became a problem. The Botels basically lived off the land and the shallow water, and when there was nothing else, Claus dipped into his sack of flour and made flour soup. Definitely not tasty, but it put something into three hungry stomachs. One day they spied a hawk flying toward them with a duck in its talons. Grabbing up handfuls of rocks, they chased the hawk all over the beach, pelting it with rocks. The hawk couldn't fly out of reach with its heavy load and one or two rocks hit their mark. At last the bird relinquished its meal and the Botels feasted on bonfire-roasted duck for supper. Another day, several red cod floated up on the beach. Claus figured there was a longliner fishing off the face of the cape, too far away to be seen, and that the crew was shaking off the red cod because they couldn't sell them. Max found some old dried-up fish skins in the shack. He cut them into thin strips with his pocket knife, and tied them together to make two fishing lines. He found some wire which he shaped into hooks, and he and Helene broke some mussels off the rocks and, using the meat for bait, the two of them went fishing off the rocks. They caught little rock cod, shiners and bullheads, which they cleaned and roasted in the fires. Much tastier than flour soup!

Children John, Willy and Max, circa 1919.

They slept in the Kyuquot's shack because it had a dirt floor, and they could keep a fire burning there all night.

Some time into their stay, the Botels started making a canoe, with just a dull old axe and no real idea of how to proceed. Otto Botel, a son born several years later, says it's a damn good thing that they never finished it as it wouldn't have been very seaworthy and there's a good chance the three of them would have drowned.

Finally, after four weeks, help came. The Kyuquot Indians noticed the smoke from the fires and, thinking someone could be burning down their trapping cabin, decided to investigate.

What a frightening sight it was to Max and Helene when they saw the Natives approaching in their large cedar war canoe! They gestured and hollered unintelligible words as they swiftly came ashore, and the children ran as fast as they could into the shelter of the forest and hid. They were sure, after hearing so many stories in Germany, that they would end up in the stew pot if caught. Meanwhile, the Kyuquot realized no one was harming their cabin, and they approached Claus and tried to talk to him. Of course Claus didn't understand their words, but he knew they were friendly and he tried

talking the kids out of the bush. It took a great deal of convincing before they would venture back out on the beach.

The Indians took them to their camp in Battle Bay that night, and treated the shipwrecked Botels exceptionally well. For supper, there was a feast of spring salmon steaks, and later a ceremony in which young Helene was made an honorary Indian princess. The family of three were given their own cabin to sleep in and real blankets on beds. What a change from their rustic beach existence!

The next day, after another ride in the war canoes, which the children enjoyed enormously, they were taken to Kyuquot. The storekeeper there gave the family some work and a shed to sleep in. They got their meals and a little cash as well. By the time the next passenger/freight ship arrived on its trip up the coast from Victoria, the Botels had enough money to pay their fares to Holberg. Imagine their surprise when they saw Claus's son John standing on deck, looking over the rail, as the boat pulled into the dock. After doing a few odd jobs in Victoria, he had decided to rejoin the family. There was no shortage of stories to be exchanged as the boat pulled out of Kyuquot and headed up Quatsino Sound.

The tired, happy group arrived home two months after they had left on their short journey to get the skiff. By then, the rest of the family had given up hope for their safe return. They had managed to feed and care for themselves. One day, after the trio had been gone for a long time and the family had been hungry for several days, Martha took the axe out of the corner of the cabin saying "a person has to eat," and with Anna's help, she butchered the cow.

The family stayed at Top Knot for five years, and through the whole time, getting enough to eat was a big challenge. They

Claus and daughter Beatrice at Julian Cove circa 1946.

lived on what the land and local water could supply—mussels and clams from the beaches, wild game and berries from the woods, a little fish from the ocean and vegetables from their garden. They were always broke. Once in a long while, they were able to sell some of their excellent potatoes and were thankful to get ninety cents for a hundred pounds. With the start of World War One, Claus was classed as an enemy alien and unable to get a job anywhere because of it. The government even sent out a man to pick up Claus's gun. The Botels and some of their neighbours in the San Josef Valley convinced the fellow that the gun was a necessity, that they needed it for protection and for food. Reluctantly, he left the gun with them.

The family checked the beaches regularly while they were at play or at work. Again and again, the ocean cast up usable objects. It was a real bonanza when chunks of paraffin were found. They made candles using string for wicks and tubes of bull kelp for molds. One year, a load of California redwood railway ties washed ashore. The family set to work and built a small cabin for the older kids to sleep in. This made for a little bit more space for Martha, Claus and the younger children in the original cabin, which even then was not roomy.

Martha and Claus, circa 1950.

Sometimes, at night, the family heard wolves howling. It made their skin creep, although they never had problems with wolves. But, cougars were occasionally a bother. One day a cougar took a chicken, and when Claus spotted it heading up a nearby tree, he quickly grabbed his gun and shot the animal. Another time, when the family was rising in the morning, they discovered the bull standing wild-eyed and snorting at the back door. They followed the bull's tracks to his favourite sleeping spot under a tree on the sandy beach. There was a massive area of scuffed-up sand, criss-crossed with bull and cougar tracks. The cougar tracks led to a tree, from which the cougar must have leaped down onto the bull. About thirty feet away from evidence of the scuffle were a set of cougar prints made by an animal leaping away in a hurry—probably with some help from the bull.

The Botels' daughter Anneliese, born in March 1916 at Top Knot, was the only child born in the five years the family spent at this remote wilderness spot. Martha had had one or two other pregnancies which terminated early, probably due to the very arduous way of life.

The family left Top Knot in 1918. The war was over, and Claus was no longer barred from seeking

Of Carl and Martha's eight surviving children, six got together for a reunion in 1994. Front row (l to r) Claus Botel (born 1912), Anneliese Hole (1916), Helene Sorenson (1902, died 1995). Back row (l to r) Alice Arnet (1918), Johanna Strom (1925), Otto Botel (1920). The two missing survivors are Beatrice Kondrat (1923) and Anna Howich (1898). Anna died at the age of 99 in 1998.
(photo courtesy Marilyn Patterson)

employment because of his enemy alien status. The family needed more money and Claus hoped to find employment in Quatsino Sound. It is likely they were also tired of the isolation and the unending struggle to live in the wilderness.

They transported some of their belongings by rowing them out in a dory. They may also have used Captain Peterson's boat, the *Cape Scott*, with which he did the mail run from Quatsino to San Josef Bay, Sea Otter Cove and Cape Scott. The family went first to Winter Harbour. They stayed for a few months in a cabin by the creek, on the east shore across from the present settlement. Next they moved to Hecate Cove in the Quatsino area and lived in a house belonging to a man named Gill, a pio-

neer of Quatsino who had returned to his homeland. During the three years the Botels lived there, two children were born, Alice in 1918 and Otto in 1920.

Claus and the two older boys, John and Max, found jobs in Port Alice helping to clear the mill site. When the work was done, they were presented with a gift—the cookhouse. It was a very large building and the condition of the gift was that it had to be moved away. The boys and their dad took the building apart. They bought a small boat, which seemed large at the time, and transported the lumber to Julian Cove, south of Drake Island. There they built a house, and the family moved to Julian Cove in the fall of 1921. It was their first nice-sized home since leaving Germany.

The soil was fertile and they grew an abundance of produce. All the family worked the garden and hay fields—including the girls, who managed fine when the fellows were away. Claus made their hay rakes and other tools whenever possible. He also made all their furniture—beds, dressers, a desk, benches and a table. Out of an old oil drum he fashioned a wood stove. When the soles of the family's gumboots were worn through, he made soles out of alder wood and attached the tops of the old gumboots. There weren't enough pairs of boots to go around, so they were shared. When the weather allowed it, the children went barefoot.

Claus and the boys found more work driving piles for the booming grounds at Holberg. Max, John and Claus started beachcombing logs, gathering them into booms of logs and selling them. With their earnings, they bought a Fordson 24-hp donkey—the first gas-powered donkey engine in Quatsino Sound. They built an A-frame and float, and took the donkey out instead of hand-logging. This method was much more productive.

Beatrice was born in 1923 and the Botels' last child, Johanna, was born in 1925. In 1936 Claus decided to move the family to Hecate Cove, where a large piece of land was available. Martha balked. She finally had a nice home and didn't want to leave it. Claus thought it over and decided they could both have what they wanted—they would take the house with them when they moved. He and the boys, with a great deal of labour, put the home on a raft, towed it to Hecate Cove and moved it up onto the land.

Claus then bought another boat and did some commercial fishing, delivering his catches in Winter Harbour. Max, John and Willy joined him. At home they sold beef, eggs and vegetables from the garden. Claus made homemade beer which he sold and traded on the side. The family still kept the hay fields at Julian Cove active and brought the hay home to Hecate Cove for the animals.

In 1946, at the age of seventy-eight, Claus broke his leg. It never healed properly, and he was on crutches until he died at eighty-five, in 1953.

During his lifetime, Claus had supported and helped raise the nine children of his first marriage, the two children of Martha's and the eight children they had together. The family's lives were mostly all work and no play. Claus's children remember some very, very tough times during their growing-up years. But all the children, girls and boys alike, grew up to be wilderness survivors who could always make do with what they had. They were excellent fishermen, hunters, trappers and gardeners, and a couple of them were good boatbuilders. They were all able to repair almost anything and did not have to be dependent on others, yet they have always been willing to help others. Their father was a strong, determined, practical man who believed in hard work and self-reliance. He could be a hard and obstinate driver, yet they also remember him as an honest man with a twinkle in his eye.◆

Booting the Big Ones Home
Log Barging on the BC Coast, 1922–1998

by David R. Conn

Since the turn of the century, getting logs from upcoast camps to southern mills has been a major task of the forest and towing industries in British Columbia. Log booms got the job done in sheltered waters, and Davis rafts (giant floating bundles of logs) in more exposed waters, but at a cost—logs were damaged and lost. Salt, sinkage, marine borers and storms all took their toll.

As logging operations moved farther upcoast from the southern sawmills, log barges gradually replaced Davis rafts for moving logs out of camps north of Johnstone Strait. Pioneering efforts at log barging began as early as 1922, when marine engineer Bill Ballantyne drew up plans for a towed vessel, resembling a military landing craft, to carry three quarters of a million board feet of timber. The barge was never built.

The 453-foot *Seaspan Forester* (formerly *Island Forester*) is the largest log barge in the world, with a capacity of 4 million board feet.
(photo courtesy Seaspan)

Laid-up sailing ships and war surplus wooden steamer hulls, called Ferris hulls, could be bought cheaply during the 1920s, and BC logging operators took advantage of that situation. *Drumrock*, a steel barque, was converted by Captain Barney Johnson of Hecate Straits Towing, and the Gibson brothers converted *Black Wolf*, a Ferris hull, to be towed by the *Lorne*.

According to W.G. Crisp, who worked on her conversion in 1924, the 329-foot *Drumrock* was the first

to put his new vessel on a run to the Queen Charlotte Islands and load spruce logs for Vancouver mills.

When the steam tug *Masset* arrived at English Bay, its crew was quick to note the large military number 13 still on *Bingamon*'s bow, and the men convinced Wingate that some work with a can of black paint was needed to improve prospects for the trip. Bill Ballantyne, who was engineer of the *Masset*, settled the discussion by saying, "You want to get there, don't you?"

Laid-up sailing ships and war surplus wooden steamer hulls could be bought cheaply during the 1920s. The 329-foot steel barque *Drumrock* was BC's first self-loading log barge. During the conversion, her four steel masts were shortened, but the lower yards were retained to support cargo booms. Each mast had a winch installed at its base. Logs were loaded through enlarged deck hatches.
(photo courtesy Vancouver Maritime Museum)

self-loading log barge. Captain Johnson had apprenticed on square-riggers like her and he hired tradesmen to alter the venerable barque to his specifications. The four steel masts were shortened, but the lower yards were retained to support cargo booms. Each mast had a winch installed at its base to load logs through enlarged deck hatches.

About the same time, Captain Walter Wingate bought a surplus steamer hull in Seattle and had it towed to Vancouver. Wingate contracted with Burrard Dry Dock to mount a 30-ton capacity derrick on rails along the hatches of the 268-foot *Bingamon*. The captain decided

The *Masset* hooked up the *Bingamon* and headed north. All went well, until two days later when tug and tow were halfway across Queen Charlotte Sound. It was blowing hard, and a series of red flares went up from the barge. As the hull pitched up and down, the travelling crane slid wildly fore and aft along the deck rails. Wingate and his bargees chased it back and forth with the lashing-down gear they had forgotten to install before leaving. The tug crew finally got *Bingamon* into *Masset*'s lee, and the crane was duly secured.

A little later, while bucking a full gale in Hecate Strait, *Masset*'s water tank burst and flooded the engine room. Tug and tow were forced to run before the wind. Then, off Triple Island, the towline parted. *Masset* struggled into Prince Rupert to get repairs, while *Bingamon* drifted into a cove near Barren Island, where the crew dropped anchor.

The vessels were reunited and finally reached Cumshewa Inlet, where *Bingamon* loaded nearly a million board feet of spruce logs. Just as the loading was completed, the crane boom collapsed. Returning south with the loaded hull in tow, *Masset* ran low on coal and barely made Vancouver. It was not an auspicious beginning for log barging, but mariners were still learning how to work with this new type of operation.

Log barges were subject to the same risks as other vessels operating along the west coast, and some were damaged or lost. *Black Wolf* hit a rock in Slingsby Channel and sank in 1926. *Drumrock* broke her back on an uncharted reef in Smith Inlet in 1927. *Bingamon* burned to the waterline near Nootka in 1928, and was towed to Victoria to be scrapped.

In his book *Bull of the Woods*, Gordon Gibson recounted the spontaneous conversion of the five-masted auxiliary schooner *Malahat* for log hauling in 1936. She had already had a colourful career, since World War One had turned the international shipping industry on its head. Built from non-strategic local softwood, the 246-foot *Malahat* and her sisters carried valuable BC lumber to desperate overseas buyers under canvas, saving precious fuel. As soon as the war ended, the big schooners became obsolete. Coal-belching steamships again took over carrying export lumber, and *Malahat* was a white elephant. She made her postwar living as a rumrunner and operated for months at a time in international waters beyond the US territorial limit. She was a mother ship, loaded with thousands of cases of liquor, which other ships and speedboats carried to the coast to be smuggled ashore. The Gibson brothers actually bought the schooner to get spare engine parts for another vessel in their haywire fleet.

While sailing her to the Charlottes in 1936, the Gibsons had some of their loggers cut out the 'tween deck beams, which created sufficient room to load the logs but weakened the ship. On arrival at Cumshewa, the crew discovered the logs awaiting them were too heavy to hoist and too long for the cargo hatches. They decided to chop down one mast and open up a 50-foot hatch, using axes and crosscut saws. The hired captain objected, so the project was completed while he was asleep. The Gibsons also built a heavy-lift cargo boom on the spot, to load 40-ton logs.

Log barges were subject to the same risks as other vessels operating along the west coast, and some were damaged or lost. In 1926, *Black Wolf* hit a rock in Slingsby Channel and sank. *(photo courtesy Vancouver Maritime Museum)*

For a time, *Malahat* was the only self-propelled, self-loading, self-unloading log vessel in the world. Later the Gibsons removed her semi-diesel engines and more masts, reducing her to a barge towed by their converted tugs. *Malahat* finally ended her career off Barkley Sound in 1944, when a deckload of spruce logs broke loose and pounded on her bulwarks, opening the hull seams.

Following a career as an offshore lumber carrier and later as a rumrunner, the 246-foot, five-masted auxiliary schooner *Malahat* was purchased by the Gibson brothers in 1936 and converted to a log carrier. For a time she was the only self-propelled, self-loading, self-unloading log vessel in the world. When this photo was taken, the Gibsons had removed her semi-diesel engines and all but two of her masts, reducing her to a barge that had to be towed by tugs. *(photo courtesy Vancouver Maritime Museum)*

Log barging offered advantages over the cumbersome Davis rafts. Barges could be towed more quickly and in heavier weather, supplying logs to the mills year round. Rafts couldn't be used during storms, when tugs and tows had to run for shelter and wait—sometimes for weeks—until the weather moderated.

On the other hand, old hulls carrying logs could be unseaworthy when lacking hatch covers, complete decks or bulkheads. Their capacity was small, loading logs through deck hatches was inefficient, log cargoes damaged wooden hulls, and crews were needed aboard to load and to steer while under tow. Clearly there was room to improve the log barge concept.

After World War Two, a new fleet of surplus vessels was available, and this helped BC towing and forest companies move ahead with log barging. Straits Towing bought four steel tank landing craft hulls (LSTs) from Burrard Dry Dock in 1945, and began the practice of carrying logs on deck, lashed between heavy steel bulwarks.

Captain Cliff Eastwood got his start as a bargee with Island Tug and Barge in 1950. His duties included taking the helm of log-carrying hulls while under tow. He crewed the *Riversdale* and *Island Forester*, both converted sailing ships, on runs to Port Alice. The wheels were original sailing ship fittings, seven feet tall. The only heat came from a wood stove in the makeshift wheelhouse. The bargees got groceries from the tugboat and cooked for themselves on board.

Captain Laurie Lusk also began his career as a bargee on the *Island Forester*. He recalls the barge had three cranes powered by a coal-fired steam donkey, and a crew of eleven men. When it was time to load at the logging camps, local fishermen were hired to come in with their boats and corral the logs in the water.

According to Jim Matthew, a marine surveyor with the Salvage Association, MacMillan Bloedel began researching log barge design during the late 1940s. The company was concerned about waste from long tows using Davis rafts, and about the time it took to offload logs from barges. Company researchers were led to the Sause brothers, who ran a small logging operation in Oregon. Iced up and desperate to get a load of logs off a flat deck barge, they had resorted to tipping the vessel, and so had pioneered side-dumping in North America.

The converted sailing ship *Island Forester* had a crew of eleven, and three cranes powered by a coal-fired steam donkey. While the barge was under tow, the only heat came from a woodstove in the makeshift wheelhouse. The barge crew got groceries from the tugboat and cooked for themselves on board.
(photo courtesy Vancouver Maritime Museum)

The technique was used in Europe for small barges hauling sand or gravel, but the brothers' application of side-dumping for logs had major consequences for the BC logging and towing industries.

In 1954, self-dumping log barges came to BC in two very different ways. Harold Elworthy arranged for Island Tug and Barge to buy several oil tankers from Venezuela for conversion to barges which would side-dump their deckloads. The shallow-draft vessels had been specially built to work on Lake Maracaibo. They had internal tanks, and they had the correct hull proportions to be partially flooded for tipping and then righted. Four were towed from Balboa to Victoria, a distance of 4,000 miles, by company tugs *Sudbury* and *Island Sovereign*.

The conversions were designed by local naval architect Robert Allan Ltd. After installation of tipping tanks, each hull could carry 1.25 million board feet of logs on deck, and dump the load in an hour. The logs were oriented athwartships, rather than fore and aft.

Cliff Eastwood served his mate's time towing some of those barges aboard coastal tugs like *Island Commander* and *Island Navigator*. He recalls, "They were quite delicate in tide; they could take a sheer and dump in the middle of a tow." Because the hulls were narrow, logs might be stacked in a single tier, which made the load unstable.

Around the same time, MacMillan Bloedel hired Robert Allan Ltd. to design a self-dumping log barge as a new type of vessel. Developed with the aid of tank testing at ship model laboratories, the resulting pair of 342-foot welded steel barges could be towed at 6.5 knots loaded or 8 knots light. Built by Burrard Dry Dock, the sisters *Powell No. 1* and *No. 2*, later renamed *Alberni Carrier* and *Powell Carrier*, became prototypes for today's fleet of purpose-built log barges, increasing efficiency and raising the technological and financial ante among lumber and towing companies.

The innovative new barges had completely flat decks with log stops fore and aft, and incorporated tipping tanks in the port sides of their hulls. Their structure was also new, with thick deck and bottom plating, plus reinforcing webs, girders and pillars within the hulls. Twin skegs provided stability, at some expense in drag. The loads were not lashed down; logs were held in place by being wedged against the log stops.

With self-dumping barges came some tricky new situations. There were "hang-ups," when the logs refused to come off, and "jackpots," when they came off in a tangle. Tug crews learned ways to cope. An extreme method with hang-ups was the "big lift"—or dynamite. Setting the charge was hazardous, as the listing barge might depart from under its load of logs at any moment. At least once, a hole was blown in the deck and the barge sank. A jackpot meant boom boats and small tugs had to go into the floating log pile for a giant game of pickup sticks, also a hazardous undertaking.

Bill Dolmage, a well-known towboat fleet operator, claimed to have been the first log barge blaster. He described the process in Ken Drushka's book about the BC towboat industry, *Against Wind and Weather*.

In the mid-1950s, self-dumping log barges made their debut. The *Powell No. 1* was one of two 342-foot welded steel barges, built for MacMillan Bloedel, that became prototypes for today's fleet of purpose-built log barges. The innovative new barges had completely flat decks, and tipping tanks were incorporated in the port sides of their hulls. The loads were not lashed down; logs were held in place by being wedged against the log stops. *(photo courtesy Vancouver Maritime Museum)*

Dolmage, who had handled explosives during the war, said he put four or five bags along the high side of a listing barge, with twenty sticks of powder in each. He connected the sticks together with cordex wiring, got well away from the barge, and detonated the charges by remote control.

By 1960, there were a dozen self-dumping log barges in operation, and barging had completely replaced Davis rafts, carrying one-third of the coastal cut. BC Forest Products' *Forest Prince* was launched that year. Equipped with two 35-ton capacity Loraine diesel cranes on buttressed towers, she was the first purpose-built self-loading, self-dumping log barge. The cranes allowed rapid loading independent of shore facilities. Since then, the distinctive silhouettes of log barges with tower cranes have become common throughout BC waters.

The year 1961 saw the last major ship conversion, which came to a premature end. M.R. Cliff Co.'s steel barge, *Log Transporter*, formerly a Great Lakes freighter, sank off Cape Mudge after only a few months' service. The cause was probably structural failure. Despite their

lower cost, ship hulls could no longer compete against the fleet of log barges operated by forestry corporations and major towing companies. The Island Tug tanker hulls were showing their age. *Island Maple* broke in half and sank in spectacular fashion off Cape Flattery in 1963, while being towed by *Sudbury*.

During the 1960s, self-loading, self-dumping log barge design became more standardized, with spoon bow, raked stern and large skegs, fitted with husky Washington pintle cranes on towers. Robert Allan Ltd. designed most of these barges. At least one log barge, the *Straits Traveler*, was equipped with a travelling crane on the afterdeck. The 369-foot *Straits Logger* was the first log barge with a capacity of two million board feet. She was followed by sisters *Rivtow Carrier* and *Island Yarder*. At the end of the decade, a new 453-foot *Island Forester* was launched as the largest log barge in the world, a title she still holds today as the *Seaspan Forester*, with a capacity of 4 million board feet.

Captain Lusk had a lot of experience with the *Straits Logger*, and respects the seaworthiness of the type: "It would take great weather if loaded properly. As long as you could tow it, you were all right." His longtime command, the Mikimiki tug *Johnstone Straits*, was the weak link. She didn't have the power to tow the *Logger* in high winds. Lacking ballast, barges could pound while running light in big seas. Another hazard was fast dumps, which could cause damage. Lusk still remembers a wild dump at Ketchikan, Alaska: "She went up so high I could see the mill underneath the hull." When the *Island Forester* was built, Captain Eastwood towed it with the *Island King*. "You had your hands full in weather and in tide," he says.

Shipyard maintenance crews were also kept busy on the log barges. Fast dumps could cause bent crane booms, and steel decks became dented and cracked from the constant impact of logs and grapples.

Towing companies had to get tugs powerful enough to tow the larger barges safely, and hustle them along at competitive speeds. In 1965, Straits Towing launched the 3,600-hp *Gibraltar Straits*. Island Tug repowered the *Island Sovereign* to handle the *Island Yarder*, and Rivtow bought and repowered a British salvage tug as the *Rivtow Lion*, with 3,200 hp. She was able to tow the *Rivtow Carrier* at 9 knots loaded. Since each tug was different, companies paired the tugs and barges that worked best together. The *Rivtow Carrier* was the first barge to have remote radio control of the diesel power plant, lighting and anchor gear on board.

While the larger, more powerful tugs made a better match with the new log barges, fleet operators also began using water or fuel ballast to stabilize the barges when running light, and running controlled dumps, which reduced damage. It was all part of the learning process in a unique operation. There were no exact precedents to follow.

Some foreign recognition of BC log barging leadership came in 1970. Robert Allan Ltd. designed a pair of 352-foot self-loading, self-dumping barges which were built in Germany and based in Sweden. They were equipped with freighter cargo cranes to handle bundled pulp logs.

Perhaps the ultimate in log barge sophistication was reached in the mid-1970s, with the design of two self-propelled, self-loading, self-dumping log carriers by

Talbot Jackson and Associates, for Kingcome Navigation. Once again parent company MacMillan Bloedel took the initiative to advance log transportation development with the 430-foot *Haida Monarch* and 398-foot *Haida Brave*, designed to combine the features of log barge and ship. Both have twin propellers with steerable nozzles, accommodation for a full crew, and the capacity to travel at 12 knots loaded. *Haida Monarch* makes a regular run to the Charlottes, while *Haida Brave* goes to Vancouver Island. These specialized vessels carry through the concept of the converted *Malahat*, though a quantum leap from her capabilities.

Modern log barges have occasionally been grounded, and have proved amenable to salvage efforts. In December 1983, *Seaspan Rigger* escaped from her tug and got stranded on an island in Barkley Sound. The accident broke her back and destroyed much of her bottom plating. The *Rigger* appeared to be on the rocks for good, but salvors hired by Seaspan found a solution. First they cut the big barge in half. Then each half was lifted on a cushion of compressed air and pulled off the rocks. The halves were patched, lashed together again and towed to Esquimalt, still floating on compressed air and without a sound bottom. The continuous deck design of log barges helped make this operation possible, as it was easy to seal the hulls to keep the air inside. Later the repaired barge halves were towed separately to Vancouver and welded back into one unit.

During the 1980s, construction costs became a major obstacle to continued progress in log barge technology. The latest generation of barges is represented by the *Seaspan Rigger* and *Rivtow Hercules*, equipped with heavy-lift hydraulic cranes and other specialized features. The construction of the "package" of *Hercules* and tug *Captain Bob* cost over $20 million.

As log loading practices have gone from loose logs to small bundles to larger bundles, barge operators have been pressured to increase crane capacity. There are now several heavy-lift crane log barges in the coastal fleet, and others are likely to be recraned to handle 50-ton bundles. However, the cost of these custom-built cranes has risen to $1 million each. It has been more affordable to upgrade existing barges by applying

Some consider the ultimate in log barge sophistication to have been reached in the mid-1970s, with the design of the 430-foot *Haida Brave* (above) and the 398-foot *Haida Monarch* (below). These are self-propelled, self-loading, self-dumping log carriers. They were designed to combine the features of log barge and ship. Both have twin propellers with steerable nozzles, full crew accommodation and the capacity to travel at 12 knots loaded. *(photos courtesy Vancouver Maritime Museum)*

The latest generation of log barges is represented by vessels such as the *Seaspan Rigger* (above) and *Rivtow Hercules* (below). Both are equipped with heavy-lift hydraulic cranes and other specialized features. Some companies believe the optimum size of barge to serve logging camps has been reached with this generation of vessels. *(photos courtesy Vancouver Maritime Museum)*

thicker decking made of higher-grade steel, which helps prevent damage from falling logs and grapples.

Operations on one of BC's self-loading, self-dumping log barges begin at a logging camp in some sheltered inlet, where hundreds of logs have been stored in special booms or "bags" ready for loading. Tug crew members anchor an empty log barge in position. The log loaders have flown in by seaplane. As former loggers, they have an intuitive knowledge of how different sizes and species of logs will load.

After stowing their gear on the tug, where they will bunk, the loaders go aboard the barge. Climbing up inside the crane towers, they start up the diesels and swing the cranes around to lift the boom boats off the barge and into the water. Then they work the grapples down among the floating timber, selecting logs or bundles and placing them on the deck. The loaders are in constant radio communication with each other and the tug crew. They pile hundreds of logs on deck in a hill-like mass, which is meant to stay put without being lashed down, yet will dump smoothly at the end of the voyage. The first tier of the load is formed with butted pairs of short logs which overhang both sides. The pile is continued with single short logs, then smaller and shorter logs. As the load is built, the head loader uses a variety of methods to check the changing metacentric height of the barge, to ensure proper stability.

In less than twenty-four hours, there are thousands of tons of timber stacked aboard the barge. The loaders are flown out, and tug and tow head south toward dumping grounds on the Lower Mainland. If the weather is good, the tow itself is uneventful.

At the dumping grounds, the tug crew gets the barge ready to dump. Then comes an awesome sight unique to British Columbia. A radioed command opens valves inside the barge hull and the barge slowly lists as sea water rushes into the tipping tanks. For some minutes, it lists toward capsize, until the load seems to be defying gravity. Very suddenly, with a roar, the barge then slides out from under the logs, restrained by lines at bow and stern. If the dump is good, the logs float in a row. The barge, freed of its load, rights itself as the tipping tanks empty. The barge is cleaned up and checked for damage. Then it is towed north to another camp, to repeat the whole process.

Over the years, the operation of log barges has done a lot to keep British Columbia forest product prices competitive on volatile world markets. Barging the logs to sawmills or pulp mills, ever more efficiently, has kept transportation costs per unit of wood low, even as tow distances increase. With costs and needs continuing to shift, it is hard to predict the future of log barges. They will evolve along with the lumber and pulp industry, as they have in the past, but they will probably not get larger. Companies believe the optimum size of barge for logging camps has been reached with the *Seaspan Rigger* and *Rivtow Hercules*.

Looking to the future, naval architect Mark Mulligan of Vancouver Shipyards commented, "Camp operators would love to put 70-ton bundles in the water." Each truckload could be bundled as a unit, minimizing log handling costs. Kingcome's marine superintendent, Tom Nixon, sees barges ranging farther north for wood and handling larger bundles. Even further in the future, he suggests, crane loading may be bypassed by the use of submersible barges, like those the oil industry uses.

Naval architect Robert G. Allan speculates that others may follow Swiftsure Towing, which has decraned the *Forest Prince* and now loads with floating derricks. Swiftsure's parent company, Fletcher Challenge, also operates a fleet of flat deck barges, loaded by means of floating cranes. Allan mentions that dryland log sorts could change log barging. Whatever the future holds for the work of getting logs from upcoast camps to southern mills, it is certain that ideas for log-carrying vessels will develop and adapt to coastal economics and conditions. As Robert G. Allan noted, "Log barges are a unique accomplishment—conceived, developed and refined in BC."◆

HIS WORLD TURNED UPSIDE-DOWN

by Duane Noyes

Mike Burke lay stunned where he had been thrown, his body battered and bruised from the impact. Above him on the ceiling, which only seconds ago had been the floor, the huge diesel motor screamed its objection to being upside down and out of lubricating oil, then finally shuddered to a grinding halt. Except for the occasional drip, drip, drip of oil or salt water, the small, dank chamber was deathly quiet.

Despite his pain, Mike struggled to his feet and peered around through the musty gloom. The chilling truth was terrifyingly obvious: he was buried alive in a steel coffin.

The 2,200-ton self-dumping log barge on which he was the first mate had somehow flipped upside down, with him trapped inside. The rusty iron crypt in which he was imprisoned now lay fifty feet deep in the frigid waters of Neroutsos Inlet, and the only way out—if there was a way out—was down.

Mike eased himself to a sitting position on the cold, wet beams of what had been the ceiling. Fortunately the emergency lighting system was still

Mike Burke was trapped inside the *Sealink Rigger* when it flipped over near Port Alice on Vancouver Island in 1995.

functional, the dim glow from its tiny bulbs casting eerie shadows on the steel walls around him. It was fear, not cold, that was making him shiver.

Mike was a skilled and seasoned mariner who had spent most of his life on the water. This particular bargeload of logs had started out no different from the hundreds of others he and the crew of the tug *Arctic Hooper* had successfully towed up and down the coast. Two days earlier, the barge *Sealink Rigger* had been loaded forty feet high from stem to stern with tons of log bundles. The tow from Iceberg Inlet to the pulp mill at Port Alice, on the west coast of Vancouver Island, had been uneventful. And on this drizzly, overcast day in August, Mike had gone aboard the barge as usual to open the tipping tank valves. These valves allow sea water to flood into the port side, tipping the load to about a 45- or 50-degree angle. All the logs slide off the barge into the water, Mike closes the valves, the water is pumped out, and barge, tug and crew are off to some other logging camp to pick up another load. It's as simple as that—at least it's supposed to be.

For some reason this particular load refused to dump. When that happens, the only alternative is to close the valves, pump out the water to level the load, fly in the loaders and unload the bundles with the huge log loading crane that is a part of the barge. That is why Mike had been below decks ten minutes ago, when the load suddenly shifted. It slid partway off and stopped, and those extra tons all on one side, combined with the weight of the water in the flooded tanks, was enough to bring about the unthinkable. The starboard side rose from the blackened sea like a monster and reared over the assist tugs helping with the dump. With a terrible groaning shudder, the barge capsized in a maelstrom of tumbling logs, broken boomsticks, flying cables and shattering machinery.

Now Mike was presumed dead, and on the surface far above, the assist boat crews continued to search frantically through the debris for his body. But Mike was not thinking of that. He was watching as cold salty water rushed into the barge through the only hatchway. Soon the chamber would be completely full. He knew he had only a few minutes to plan an escape and carry it out before his air supply was depleted. He tried to swim through the hatch but the current was too strong. Abandoning his life jacket and shoes, he again dove down through the hatch, only to be forced back. Even if he did get out, he realized, he would have to swim underwater along twenty feet of gangway and through another small engine room before getting out. Once out he would have to navigate through a tangle of ropes, lines, twisted metal and who knew what else before getting clear of the inverted deck. Then, once free of the barge, he would somehow have to get through the heavy logs and other flotsam and jetsam that would be choking the surface after the accident. Mike doubted very much that he could hold his breath for the three or four minutes it would take him to reach safety, but it was his only option.

The water flowing into the barge had slowed enough that on his third attempt Mike was able to swim against the current. But he had only gone as far as the small engine room when his lungs began to feel as if they would explode. With more than a hundred feet to go, he knew he wouldn't make it, but turning back was futile as well. Miraculously, there was a three-foot air pocket in the engine room. It too was slowly disappearing, but it could save his life.

Three times Mike filled his lungs with air before diving out through the doorway and trying to find his way to freedom. Three times he encountered only endless darkness and was forced to return to his rapidly diminishing air pocket. He had no way of knowing which way to turn to get to the surface. His fourth attempt would be his last—the precious air supply had been reduced to only inches. He gulped what might very well be his last breath and dove out the door.

At about the same time Mike was preparing for his last dive, the tide changed, and it cleared the surface just as another twist of fate occurred. The sun, which hadn't shone for days, broke through the heavy cloud cover and cut down through the murky gloom like a lighthouse beacon. Mike had the guidance he needed. With lungs aching and sore muscles straining, he plunged forward through the maze of tangled junk toward the light and followed it to the surface. The astonished tug crew dragged a sputtering, gasping Mike on board as the sun slipped back behind the clouds.

Some people would like to be lucky enough to win a big lottery, others want the good fortune to be famous, still others crave the good luck that brings health, happiness, power and status or some combination of these. Mike is not much different from his fellow human beings, except that he seems satisfied with nothing more than tide changes, small air pockets and sunlight overhead—lots and lots and lots of sunlight overhead.◆

They Don't Make 'Em Any More Department
Fisherman Hank McBride

by Michael Skog

Hank McBride has been involved in the fisheries since the late thirties when he began his career on the decks of his uncle's boat. He is perhaps best known as the skipper of his last boat, the ninety-eight-foot steel dragger *Gail Bernice* (now the *Viking Storm*), but during his life he has harvested a lot more than bottom fish. He started out fishing for salmon, then skippering salmon tenders (packers) for BC Packers, and began trawling in his later days.

Hank well remembers his first trip up the coast in 1937. His folks sent him up to Rivers Inlet on one of the Union Steamships when he was fourteen years old, so that he could work with his uncle on a fishing boat.

No sooner was he aboard than a troop of rowdy loggers adopted him. As he sat with them awaiting his first meal, he was awed by their reckless debauchery. They bellowed loudly, gestured grandly and drank heavily, including Hank in the conversation and making him feel like he belonged in their world. "I'm feeling pretty good because I'm one of them," he says

Although he says he's retired, Hank still manages to get a bit of fishing in each year as a relief skipper.

An early postcard showing Namu. The fishermen's floats are to the left and one of the many bunkhouses to the right. The bunkhouses provided modest accommodation for the hundreds of BC Packers seasonal employees. The highest dwellings built onto the hill above the bunkhouse were cabins for married office workers. The boardwalks were essential to carry pedestrian traffic over the rocky shores and inland bogs.

years later. Finally the food came and Hank and his companions flew at the feast. Unfortunately, one of Hank's dinner companions had gone a little heavily on the apéritifs and, in Hank's words, "the silly son of a bitch pukes all over the table. All over his plate, my plate. I was hungrier than a bear and thought, Oh shit. After that I was still hungry. And then the skipper walked in."

The captain observed the spectacle unfolding over at the loggers' table and shouted "Get that kid out of there. Put him at my table." Hank couldn't believe his luck. "Well now I get to sit at the skipper's table, with the chief engineer, the skipper, the radio operator and all the officers, see…then, o'course, the engineer, he says, 'Laddie, you'll come down to the engine room to see the engine.' That's just what I wanted to hear, so I sez 'You bet!'" The captain, not to be outdone by one of his subordinates, extended an invitation to visit the bridge of

the large, classy vessel any time Hank wanted. Finally, the radio operator followed suit. "I had the run of the ship," Hank grins.

As it happened, there was another boy on board, about Hank's age. "He was rich—he had a tutor. So me being a kind of friendly type—I walk up to him and goes 'Hi.' He frowned at me, sneered, and walked off. Me and my rubber boots, my dungarees, and one shirt—didn't impress him one bit. I remember thinking, 'son of a bitch!' Then I went into the wheelhouse and he followed. The old skipper, he kicked him out." The memory of the little snob getting his comeuppance still brings on a deep belly laugh.

Payback time makes Hank think of another time when his boat was unloading bottom fish. When time came to deliver, the boat made its way to the Glenrose Cannery, which lay at the south end of Annacis Island in the Fraser River. It was owned in part by a fellow named

Dougal Bartlett, "Old Dougal—quite religious old Dougal Bartlett—just a tiny little guy," Hank remembers. Hank figured Bartlett didn't have the best rapport with his men, clinging to a puritanical work ethic and always dressing in a white pressed shirt with collar and tie. His shore crew thought him an insufferable, self-righteous pain in the butt who milked every misdeed for its moral lessons. On that day a group of fishermen had gathered for some recreation. Among them was an old-timer Hank knew as Old Nelson, who in addition to being a fisherman was also part owner of the Glenrose. "This old Nelson, he was a real old bugger. They were all down at the boat, you know, drinking. And of course Bartlett comes down and he sees them out there, and sees that everybody down at the cannery, they're all drunk. The whole goddamn cannery was drunk, it didn't matter who you were. Dougal comes down and he starts to squawk at everybody sitting there drinking, not doing anything."

It was a weekend, and the fishermen had nothing to do while they waited for their fish to be unloaded, but Bartlett went on and on. At the zenith of his sermon, Old Nelson decided to remind him of the days before his religious conversion. "Jesus Christ, Dougal," he bellowed, "remember years ago when you and I was young at Ewen's Cannery, when you used to make silver dollars out of seine leads, and shine 'em up and give 'em to the klootches for a piece of tail?" Whether or not it was true didn't matter—the crowd surrounding the men were convinced by Bartlett's ghostly complexion, and they enjoyed a good guffaw at his expense.

"Old Dougal, he was all embarrassed," says Hank as he jiggles with laughter. Then he becomes solemn, remembering that Bartlett was also "a fine old gentleman. He worked hard all his life." Bartlett eventually sold his share of the enterprise to Canadian Fishing Company and bought two tickets for an around-the-world cruise. As he stepped up the gangplank with his wife, he dropped dead. Bartlett's wife never recovered from the shock and spent the rest of her life in an institution. The Glenrose, Bartlett's sole legacy, is still there and still owned by Canadian Fish. Only now the building serves as a storage locker.

Hank worked hard and became a well-respected skipper for BC Packers. One night he was travelling to Vancouver with a full load, accompanied by another boat, the *Mermaid*, skippered by a man named Jack. It was late at night, and the only aids to navigation were lighthouses, the lights on their boats and the glow from shoreside communities. As they chugged along, Hank and Jack talked to each other on the radio, keeping each other awake. They were heading into Johnstone Strait and approaching Alert Bay on their left-hand side when Hank noticed another boat. It seemed to be heading across the channel toward Port McNeill, and Hank realized with alarm that it was on a collision course with the *Mermaid*. Hank held his breath and prepared for the worst as the two sets of lights slowly converged, "getting closer and closer and closer and closer and closer till the two boats merged into one, and then they parted and each went its own way."

It must have been a week later when a group of tendermen were tied up in Namu waiting for fish and Jack, who had recovered from the shock enough to talk about it, treated them to a rant about the near miss. "S-s-s-stupid son of a bitch come out of Alert Bay—pretty near hit me!"

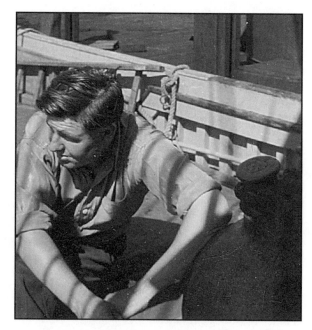

Hank McBride, at leisure on the back deck of his salmon tender, the *Sharon M*, c. 1950.

This prompted another skipper to describe a similar event that had happened to him. "Stupid son of a bitch comin' down the channel pretty near hit me the other morning!" Hank couldn't help noticing how much the two tales had in common. "The two guys finally get to talking," he says, "and they figure out, Jesus Christ, it's each other!" The two skippers got so mad they nearly came to blows. Hank still laughs about it.

Another of Hank's favourite stories starts on a fine summer night when he and a highliner friend of his named John were partying on the boats in port. John went to the rail, retched violently and "puked out his teeth." The poor man could only watch them sink to the bottom. Soon afterwards the two friends got together once again, this time in the more civil environment of John's living room, with their respective spouses. While they sipped coffee and sampled cookies, John's son, a cute ten-year-old, asked the guests if they wanted to hear how his dad had lost his false teeth. The boy recounted the heroic life-and-death tale that had unfolded the week before. High seas and gale force winds had mercilessly pummelled his father's boat, and suddenly one of the savage waves had heaved the boat so far to the side that a skiff broke free of its lashings and rammed the back of his brave daddy's head, knocking out his teeth, which were quickly swallowed by the sea.

Hank and John exchanged glances. For a man who appreciates a joke, it was a long moment and an enormous temptation. Yet Hank resisted. "Oh ya, I remember now," he said. The memory of it still gives him a good laugh.

In the late forties, Hank and his wife Ruth met in Namu, where she worked at the only cafe in town. It was just the beginning of Namu's golden age. The Namu operation saw a great deal of activity, and required a huge number of seasonal workers who came from all over. Most of them were young, eager people of all races who worked together all day but socialized only within their own groups. There were separate bunkhouses for men, women, married, single, European, Native, Chinese and Japanese workers. Married couples occupied a section of town called Tunerville, consisting of small cottages, but the single workers slept two to a room in enormous bunkhouses. For consenting adults, the social calendar

Inside the Namu Cafe, where Ruth McBride worked. She is behind the counter, at the fountain, with a scarf tying back her hair. The cafe was a popular meeting place and nearly always busy during the fishing season.

Ruth McBride sitting with Hank's father Bert, aboard the *Sharon M.* This photograph was taken at Wadhams Cannery in Rivers Inlet, during the Rivers Inlet salmon run. Typical packer paraphernalia, including scales to weigh fish, can be seen in the stern, opposite the dory.

featured weekly dances at the far side of town and the local bowling alley provided further distraction. Namu was the ideal place for hormonal expression. Most romances were of the respectable variety. Competition was fierce—men overwhelmingly outnumbered women. "You had to be pretty on the ball to keep a woman in Namu at that time."

Hank remembers fondly one early morning when he stole away to visit a woman during the dark hours before work. As he tiptoed back to his boat in the first light of dawn, he encountered another man, also carrying his shoes and trying to be silent as he moved along the wooden promenade. This man was an office lackey, universally unpopular among fishermen, as Hank puts it, "a hoity-toity son of a bitch." The two men exchanged a nod of recognition and continued along their way. But just a few yards later, they were both startled by the cheerful voice of "Mac" Maclean, the camp manager, wishing them both a loud "Morning, boys!"

Hank was delighted, but the other gentleman was horrified. Not only had he been caught with a smoking gun, he had been lumped into the same category as a lowly boat person.

Namu was accessible only by fish boat, packer or coastal steamship. The isolation often contributed to reckless behaviour, as if the camp's physical distance from civilization was also a moral one. "You didn't have to go far to get in a goddamn fight." Fuelled by booze and boredom, fighting became an integral part of life in Namu. It was a tough neighbourhood when everyone got boozed up. The non-Natives threatened to kill all the Natives and the Natives vowed to kill all the non-Natives. There was continual talk of racial wars. In practice, however, the lines of combat were not so neatly drawn. Both Natives and non-Natives got just as much pleasure fighting amongst themselves as with each other.

As the province had Judge Begbie to keep order in its untamed years, Namu had Mac Maclean. Hank remembers this fellow as a respected manager, a good friend and a legendary disciplinarian. The delicate peace in Namu was maintained entirely by Mac, who was the "head honcho" and knew everyone personally. Perhaps more important, they knew him—and his legendary mean side. "Boy, was old Mac tough," says Hank.

Inevitably, people sometimes exercised bad judgment by challenging Mac Maclean to a scrap. Usually the fellow was drunk, otherwise he might have thought better of it. Hank recalls being in a machine shop one day when the camp testosterone was at high tide, and an ornery machinist named Bill picked up a hammer and began smacking it into the palm of his hand, hollering "Where's that goddamn Maclean? Where the hell is he? I'll fix him up."

With the perfect timing that was characteristic of Mac, he chose that moment to rear around the corner of the machine shed. Fortunately for Bill, his position was considered valuable: Mac only put him in the hospital for a few days. This was quite charitable as Mac was rumoured to have torn men's ears off for less.

Namu did have provincial police officers, but they were ineffectual. The only real law and order there was

The famous Mac Maclean, (right) manager of the BC Packers Namu plant. His fists were legendary among the young fellows, including Hank. In their minds, Mac was a tough guy and a hero—which could not be readily observed in his kind smile. Hank remembers the man next to Mac as another fine fellow, but he doesn't remember his name.

Maclean. According to Hank, who wouldn't say no to a good party, there were times when the whole town was drunk and fighting and the police never left their boat. "They were scared to," says Hank. One morning after a town-wide brawl, Mac woke him up and asked him to go with him down to the police vessel. Mac was livid—his whole town had nearly been torn apart the night before by revelers. "He kicked the side of the boat," Hank says. "Boom, Bong, Boom! The cop poked out his head and Mac said, 'Get back inside and get out of here. Don't want you around here—you useless bunch of bastards.'"

Hank remembers another evening in Namu, a notorious Saturday night. It was about 9:00 p.m. when he nosed his packer into the dock. "My gang was sober," he says, "we were the only sober ones in town." Namu was already blind with celebration—all the fish had been delivered and there was no opening until late the next evening. But all was not good fun. There had been an altercation in which, as Hank puts it, "Somebody ran a fish pugh through somebody's guts. Run right up to the hilt." The pugh, a pole with a spike on the end for spearing fish, was none too sanitary and the man needed

medical attention. Mac Maclean had an old rumrunner with an enormous aircraft engine. It was called the *Black Hawk* and could do 40 knots. Mac, who was also partying that evening, entrusted its operation to the only skipper in town with a clear head. Hank was instructed to take the pugh to the hospital in Bella Bella and get it removed, for its owner needed it back. "I opened up the throttle," Hank says. "Forty-some knots up that goddamn Fitz Hugh Sound." Wind-induced tears slid across Hank's cheeks as he roared up the channel listening to the soft moans of his passenger, who lay beside him bleeding from the belly. The pugh was safely returned to its owner.

Hank is now officially retired, but finds fishing about as easy to give up as he does telling stories. He misses life at sea and is easily induced to go back on board whenever somebody needs a relief skipper. The old skipper doesn't find the modern industry compares very well to the one he knew. In his view, the proliferation of new government rules and regulations relating to the fishery have spoiled this last frontier, where a person could once be entirely in charge of his own destiny.◆

Under Fire and Under Pressure
West Coast Shipbuilders in World War II

by Vickie Jensen with Arthur McLaren

The steel shipbuilding industry in British Columbia has undergone plenty of ups and downs, but the most powerful impact on the industry was World War II. Small naval vessels were ordered and built early on, but the war was primarily a battle to control ocean transport, and it gave rise to an increased need for merchant cargo ships.

In the early years of the war, enemy submarines and aircraft took a toll of forty to eighty merchant ships every month. Despite new construction from British yards, the transfer of ships and crews from Norwegian, Danish, Dutch and Greek merchant fleets, and the release of World War I vessels from the American reserves, it was obvious that an enormous amount of merchant tonnage must be replaced if Britain was to survive. The British government had already purchased a number of older US merchant vessels from the 1920s, and for new construction, the Ministry of War Transport sent a team of shipbuilders and engine builders to the USA and Canada. They came armed with drawings for a 9,300-ton coal-burning cargo steamer made of steel.

The drawings were prepared by the North Sands yard of Joseph L. Thompson & Sons Ltd.; hence the wartime cargo vessel became known as the North Sands ship. The design was similar to that of hundreds of British tramp steamers and presented a simple, efficient ship capable of carrying bulk, baled and deck cargo. The design, which became the basis of all the emergency "Liberty" and "Ocean" ships produced in the USA and the "Fort" and "Park" ships built in Canada, called for a riveted shelter deck vessel with machinery amidships.

The lines incorporated "V" rather than "U" sections forward and a "canoe" stern. The hull was an easy form to build, requiring no furnace plates. The Americans kept the identical hull form, but adopted welded construction. Canadian practice was to rivet the longitudinal seams and weld the transverse butts.

By late 1940, the British government had ordered eighty North Sands ships—sixty to be built in the USA and twenty in Canada. The Canadian order saw twelve assigned to the St. Lawrence yards and eight to Burrard Dry Dock in North Vancouver. Shortly afterward, the US government placed orders for an additional 100 North Sands ships, to be owned by the US Maritime Commission but built in Canada and delivered to the British Ministry of War Transport under the terms of the US Lease Lend Act. Later, ships were built for the Canadian government account. Some were loaned to the British Ministry of War Transport, while others were delivered to the Park Steamship Company, a Canadian Crown corporation.

The ships built for Britain in American yards had the prefix "Ocean" in their names; those built in Canada had the prefix "Fort." Canadian-built and -operated ships were assigned the suffix "Park." All of the Canadian vessels were paid for by the British government and transferred to the Ministry of War Transport. The Ministry assigned each ship to a British shipping company which would operate it. Between 1942 and 1945, 320 cargo ships were constructed in Canada—some 255 of them in BC.

By the summer of 1941, some twenty-two shipbuilding berths had been prepared in seven steel shipyards in

West Coast Shipbuilders yard was located on the south shore of False Creek in Vancouver, just east of what is now the Cambie Street Bridge. This photo was taken looking north from 1st Avenue. Hamilton Bridge was adjacent to the shipyard. West Coast was one of seven BC shipyards producing 10,000 ton steel merchant ships during World War II.

the province: Burrard Dry Dock (North Vancouver), North Vancouver Ship Repairs Ltd. (North Vancouver), Burrard South Yard (Vancouver Harbour, south shore), West Coast Shipbuilders (Vancouver, False Creek), Victoria Machinery Depot (Victoria, outer harbour), Yarrows Limited (Esquimalt) and Prince Rupert Dry Dock Ltd. (Prince Rupert). During 1940–41, the early naval shipbuilding program employed about 1,800 men, who learned basic shipbuilding skills while constructing 190-foot patrol vessels (later designated Corvettes), 180-foot steam, twin-screw minesweepers (Bangors) and 118-foot wooden motor launches (Fairmiles). But the expanding merchant shipbuilding program required twelve times that many production employees, and altogether the seven yards employed some 25,000 men and women.

Shipyard production was only part of the wartime story. An additional 5,000 workers were employed in manufacturing components. All boilers, steering gear, winches, windlasses, masts, shafting, etc. were manufactured in BC. Steel came from three mills in eastern Canada, engines were built by three eastern Canadian firms and pumps were produced by the machine shops of the gold mines in northern Ontario. Before the start of the war, Canada had been a producer of raw materials; now the country was being transformed into an industrialized society.

Delivery of ships started in March 1942, and by July, the combined output of the Vancouver yards was an astounding two new ships per week. This level of production was maintained through 1942 and 1943. When the Battle of the Atlantic turned in favour of the Allies, shipbuilding was cut back and deliveries extended to one vessel per month in each of the Vancouver yards. In the latter part of 1943, when there was a critical demand for tankers, twelve ships of the standard design were built with tanks instead of holds. By 1944 the demand for cargo ships had lessened, and the western Canadian shipbuilding effort was directed to the war in the Far East. The final wartime program was the construction of fifteen Type "B" China Coasters. None of these 214-foot 'tween deck steamers was complete at war's end, so all were taken over by private owners.

W.D. McLaren and his son T.A. (Arthur) McLaren share a common work history at West Coast Shipbuilders, one of the seven BC yards that built North Sands ships during the war. The J. Couglan & Sons shipyard on the south shore of False Creek in Vancouver had been destroyed by fire in 1923, and adjacent to it was Hamilton Bridge, a structural steel building plant owned by the Walkem family. Peacetime construction pursuits such as bridges and office buildings were put on hold as soon as war broke out; the Walkems set up a modern 4-berth shipyard on the Couglan site at First Avenue and Columbia Street and named it West Coast Shipbuilders.

The owners of the new yard then opened negotiations with Wartime Merchant Shipping for a share of the North Sands ships, but they were told to stand by while the "established" yards received orders. Some of the existing builders opined that there was not enough labour to man another yard. West Coast's directors argued that the Hamilton Bridge company next door was much better equipped to fabricate steel than any of the existing shipyards, and that with commercial bridge building at a wartime halt, the plant was operating at less than 10 percent capacity. Their logic won out. Arthur McLaren recalls:

Although it was never written down, the federal government at that time was also concerned about labour stability. The steel shipyards were heavily unionized with agreements for every trade. Burrard Dry Dock had twenty-two separate agreements with steelworkers, shipwrights, machinists, pipefitters, coppersmiths, crane operators, etc., with new employees being recruited daily. So the federal government, through Wartime Merchant Shipping, offered West Coast Shipbuilders orders for North Sands ships, provided they kept an open shop agreement. This challenge was accepted.

Of course, we paid the wages and honoured the same terms of the union agreement as the other yards, but ours was the open shop. This matter of the open/closed shop was seen as a holy war by some. As a result, my father was portrayed as a rabid anti-unionist. He was not. He was merely carrying out his orders.

A week after completing his engineering studies at UBC in 1941, Arthur McLaren went to work as a shipbuilder—but not before trying to enlist in the armed services.

During the war, all the young guys eighteen to thirty years old either enlisted or were conscripted into the services. So it

Hull 107 (*Fort Slave*) under construction at West Coast Shipbuilders, showing girders and deck beams. During 1942 and 1943, the four Vancouver shipyards collectively delivered two 10,000 ton freighters every week.

was the men over thirty, basically, who made up the crews working in the shipyards. I got drafted myself and spent a whole day down in Little Mountain barracks, but they kicked me out and sent me home because I can only see with one eye. I reminded the officer that Nelson only had one eye, but he said Nelson started out with two good eyes. So that was it for volunteering with the Navy. And it turned out the Army wasn't interested either, so I went to work for West Coast Shipbuilders. They were just starting up, and my first job was to help lay out the yard so that four of the 10,000-ton wartime freighters could be built at the same time.

In about 1943, the Walkems sold out to Frank Ross and Victor Spencer. They bought the shipyard as well as the assets of Hamilton Bridge and brought the two False Creek firms under common ownership. W.D. McLaren, who had been general manager of West Coast Shipbuilders, was asked to continue with that company and handle Hamilton Bridge as well. His son Arthur also stayed on.

Prior to 1939, shipyards, shops and foundries all worked a forty-four-hour week, which meant five weekdays and Saturday morning. Wages in heavy industry in the Vancouver/Victoria area for tradesmen (machinists, boilermakers, moulders) employed fairly steadily under shop conditions was 75 cents per hour prior to World War II. Helpers received 50 cents per hour. Those carpenters, riveters, and shipwrights employed in outside work subjected to inclement weather earned 90 cents per hour, with specialists getting 67 cents. At the beginning of the naval shipbuilding program in 1940, wages of 90 cents per hour were established for all tradesmen, with a rate of 67 1/2 cents for unskilled workers. In 1942, rising living costs were recognized by the government, and a cost-of-living bonus of 10 cents per hour was added to all wages.

Arthur recalls that after the attack on Pearl Harbor in December 1941, Ottawa instructed Canadian shipyards to carry out continuous production, twenty-four hours per day, seven days a week. Each employee was to work eight hours per day, six days a week, with one day off per week, but not necessarily Sunday. Maintaining the seven-day production week was extremely difficult at a time when the Lord's Day Act was enforced. No shopping or commercial activities were permitted on Sundays. For many employees, Sundays were for church attendance and family activities. For some, Sunday was a day of rest following a bacchanal Saturday night.

At that time, union agreements were based on a forty-four-hour week. Men were now told to work forty-eight hours, so the additional four hours were paid at time and a half. Thus, the weekly wage was based on fifty hours' pay. This gave a tradesman $45 per week (later on $50 per week). For most, this was a bonanza compared to pre-war wages.

In the early days of World War II, tradesmen were pursued with offers of employment. But every morning there were also some two dozen men standing at the gates, waiting to be employed. These men usually were not tradesmen. They came from farms, logging camps and mines. Many had not found employment during the Depression. Others had left mundane, low-paying jobs, hoping for advancement. This was the raw material we had to work with in order to produce, if not tradesmen, then at least specialists who could build ships. The task was not so much to find workers as to fit them into a productive role.

West Coast Shipbuilders' first ship was definitely the toughest to build and launch—and the one that caused the hardest feelings. The keel of No. 101 was laid in August 1941; six months later—on March 8, 1942—it was launched, with delivery in May. The nine-month building period was governed by the six months it took to build and equip the yard, the lack of steel, holdups in the supply of templates, and the learning time necessary for all employees and supervisors.

By February 1942, the yard was under heavy stress to get the first hull launched. Hulls Nos. 102, 103 and 104 were all under construction and rapidly catching up. Hamilton Bridge had already fabricated half the steel for Hull No. 105, which was to follow No. 101 on the berth. A launching at the earliest possible date was imperative, but there were still no deckhouses erected on the first hull except the boundary bulkheads of the engine casing. Since it was apparent that deckhouse construction would have to be undertaken after the hull was afloat, all the plating stiffeners and beams for this construction were dropped helter-skelter on the upper deck.

The drawing of the deckhouse, issued by the builders of the original ship, had been done on a scale of a quarter inch to the foot. This was rather small to reveal clearly all the steel work detail and to include the markings for plates, frames, beams, etc. Furthermore, this particular drawing was difficult to decipher since it had been blueprinted from a sepia print of the original tracing. With the clarity of the drawing compromised, deciphering the data was indeed a challenge.

After launching, attention was given to shipping the three boilers and main engine. The piles of deckhouse steel were picked over, but the whole problem remained a Chinese puzzle. A week went by with no action on the deckhouses. The erection crew stood around as though waiting for guidance from some mystic spirit.

In those days, the yard ran continuously on a three-shift basis. The day shift was fully manned by senior and older men. Younger men with less experience but more get-up-and-go ran the afternoon shift, and the graveyard shift was for catching up.

One particular afternoon, we assembled gangs to blitz the deckhouses on Hull No. 101. The plan of attack was to retrieve the coaming bars for the deckhouses from the tangled piles of steel dumped on the deck. These would be bolted to the upper deck, flange up, thus establishing a datum for further erection. Next we'd tackle the look-out plates that formed the deckhouse sides. These were relatively small plates about eight by eight feet, with seams on every third stiffener. A lot of the house sides, subdivision bulkheads, etc. could be manhandled into place. A crane was used for handling deck beams and deck plating.

Using a gang of some forty fitters and ten welders, we started at 4:00 p.m. and worked through to 4:00 a.m. During that time we managed to erect 60 percent of the six deckhouses—indeed an overnight wonder.

In the course of erecting the steelwork, the pile of plates and angles was diminished and the task of locating a given plate or steel section became much less arduous. The day shift erectors who had been baffled were now in a position to continue and complete the deckhouse structures. Within two more days, deckhouse steelwork was completely erected, ready for welding and rivetting. This exercise was a challenge to teams of younger men working on their first ship. They tackled the job with great enthusiasm, knowing it was vital that deckhouses be complete for joiner and electrical work to proceed. Nonetheless, the overnight wonder caused bad feelings amongst the senior men on the day shift to whom the work was originally entrusted. They felt humiliated that a crew of young men had done on one twelve-hour shift what they had failed to get started in one week. As Arthur sums it up:

Should we have consulted with the seniors first, I doubt such parley would have made any difference. We were a bunch of smart alecks who had gone out of our way to embarrass older, experienced men. We didn't apologize. There was a war on and ships were being sunk at twice the rate of replacement. We had cleared a stoppage on the building of Hull No. 101!

Each subsequent West Coast ship, starting with Hull No. 105, was turned out from keel to launching in eight

Hull 141 (*Atwater Park*), being launched at West Coast Shipbuilders. She was one of 225 10,000 ton cargo ships built in BC for the war effort.

on one ship during its passage out of False Creek.

We always made the run from the east end of False Creek to open sea at English Bay on Sundays, so as to cause the least inconvenience to traffic held up by opening the various swing span bridges. On this particular Sunday, we had cleared False Creek and were sailing toward First Narrows. The army had installed a coastal defence gun at Ferguson Point in Stanley Park, midway between False Creek and the First Narrows. As we proceeded, a signalling lamp at the gun emplacement rattled out a speedy Morse code message. Those of us on the ship's bridge asked, "What's up?" There was another unintelligible dash of code, then another. Finally there was a puff of smoke, a scream through the air and a splash in the water about a quarter of a mile ahead of us—all quickly followed by the explosion of a gun firing!

We had an Aldis Lamp on board, so somebody who at least understood Morse code tapped out, very slowly, "What's the matter?" The reply came back flashing at a mile a minute. So our Aldis man tapped back, requesting the sender to signal slowly. That did the job. Back came the request, painfully slow: "What ship is that?" We showed our name board and that was that. End of story

One of Burrard Dry Dock's ships was not so lucky. Returning from sea trials, the vessel was similarly challenged from a gun emplacement at the north side of First Narrows, under the Lion's Gate Bridge. A warning

weeks. From keel to delivery took only twelve and a half weeks. With the second series of hulls, West Coast workers delivered a new ship through the False Creek bridges every second Sunday until the program eased off. Crews in the other three Vancouver yards met the same schedule, and from mid-1942 to late 1943, two new ships per week were dispatched from the Port of Vancouver.

Under wartime regulations, no name or any other form of identification could be exhibited on a ship. Atop the wheelhouse on each side of the rails was a heavy board bearing the ship's name. This board was hinged so that when it was folded, the top half covered the lower portion and the name was obliterated. Arthur McLaren recalls one very alarming event involving these boards that occurred

Hull 127 (*Fort Boise*) during sea trials. At the top of the photo is the old lighthouse at the mouth of the Capilano River, adjacent to First Narrows and Vancouver Harbour.

10,000 TON CARGO SHIP OUTPUT FROM BC SHIPYARDS DURING WORLD WAR II	
Burrard Dry Dock North Vancouver & Vancouver Yards	111
West Coast Shipbuilders False Creek	55
North Van Ship Repairs North Vancouver	54
Victoria Machinery Depot Victoria	20
Prince Rupert Dry Dock Prince Rupert	13
Yarrows Ltd. Esquimalt	2
Total	255

shot ricocheted off the surface of the water and actually punctured the hull of the brand new cargo ship. The vessel was beached on the sand bank on the north side of First Narrows. Fortunately, it was refloated with only minor damage.

"So," Arthur concludes, "if you ask if I've ever been under fire, I'd have to say yes, but presumably only from friendly forces!"◆

Vickie Jensen and Arthur McLaren are collaborating on a book that chronicles four generations of McLaren shipbuilders and the history of British Columbia's steel shipbuilding industry.